God wants you healed in spirit, soul, and body. Katie Souza has discovered the importance of soul healing, as wounding in the soul produces adverse symptoms in many areas of life, including physical infirmity, relationship problems, and even curses. In *Healing the Wounded Soul*, Katie skillfully leads you on a comprehensive journey through the Scriptures and reveals practical steps to experiencing the healing of the soul through Christ's *dunamis* power. Many have been profoundly set free in every area of their lives through her profound teachings on this subject. I am convinced you will be too.

—Dr. Patricia King
Patricia King Ministries
www.xpministries.com

Healing the Wounded Soul is a cutting-edge, groundbreaking work on the ministry of healing written by a radically committed Christian woman who is fearless in her pursuit of God and healing for herself and others. She has plumbed the depth of her own personal suffering and risen again on the wings of God's love and the transforming power of Christ's work on the cross to lead a new generation out of addictions, violence, anger, fear, and disease and into wholeness and life!

This book is experimental in the best and highest sense. Katie has taken God at His Word and put it to the test in every hurting, broken place in her life. This book is revelatory because out of these faith experiments Katie has gained great understanding about life and the Scriptures that others have forgotten, lost, or missed.

By the call of God her wounded soul became a laboratory of discovery for all hurting people because we comfort others with the same comfort with which we have been comforted (1 Cor. 1:4). This book is new wine; in it she shares many neglected biblical truths, along with vast insight into destructive human behavior patterns, that will provide Jehovah Rapha a powerful platform to heal you of every sickness and every disease.

Katie Souza is a friend of mine, and I assure you she embodies what she teaches. I am confident you will find the God who heals in this book. Embrace these principles as she has, and you too can gain newness of life, just as God always intended.

—JOAN HUNTER
AUTHOR/HEALING EVANGELIST
WWW.JOANHUNTER.ORG

The Scripture teaches us in Ephesians 4 that God gives to the church both teachers and prophets for the equipping of the saints for the work of the ministry. Some of these people are themselves gifts to the body of Christ. Katie Souza is one such gift from God. In this amazing book, *Healing the Wounded Soul*, Katie shares rare razor-sharp insights into the heart of God and unlocks hidden mysteries from the kingdom of heaven to help you achieve all that the Lord is calling you to do. The revelatory teachings in this book can truly transform your life as you allow the Spirit and the Word to heal your soul! This anointed book is a must-read for every believer and ministry leader in the body of Christ.

—KEVIN BASCONI
KING OF GLORY MINISTRIES INTERNATIONAL
AUTHOR OF VISITATIONS OF ANGELS AND OTHER SUPERNATURAL
EXPERIENCES SERIES
WWW.KINGOFGLORYMINISTRIES.ORG

HEALING THE WOUNDED SOUL

HEALING THE WOUNDED SOUL

Katie Souza

CHARISMA
HOUSE

Most CHARISMA HOUSE BOOK GROUP products are available at special quantity discounts for bulk purchase for sales promotions, premiums, fund-raising, and educational needs. For details, write Charisma House Book Group, 600 Rinehart Road, Lake Mary, Florida 32746, or telephone (407) 333-0600.

HEALING THE WOUNDED SOUL by Katie Souza
Published by Charisma House
Charisma Media/Charisma House Book Group
600 Rinehart Road
Lake Mary, Florida 32746
www.charismahouse.com

Cover design by Studio Gearbox
Design Director: Justin Evans

Visit the author's website at www.expectedendministries.org.

Library of Congress Cataloging-in-Publication Data:
An application to register this book for cataloging has been submitted to the Library of Congress.
International Standard Book Number: 978-1-62999-190-0
E-book ISBN: 978-1-62999-447-5

While the author has made every effort to provide accurate telephone numbers and Internet addresses at the time of publication, neither the publisher nor the author assumes any responsibility for errors or for changes that occur after publication.

Names and details of incidents in this book have been changed, except those for which permission has been granted. Any similarity between the names and stories, where changes have been made, in this book and individuals known to readers is purely coincidental.

17 18 19 20 21 — 9 8 7 6 5 4 3 2 1
Printed in the United States of America

To Mom,
my husband, Bobby,
all my staff,
every friend and partner of this ministry,
and most of all my Lord.

CONTENTS

FOREWORD

GOD USED KATIE Souza to save my life! In 2013 the enemy attacked me extremely hard, and I went through several years of sickness and affliction. By gaining access to my wounded soul, the enemy was able to break down my body, almost resulting in my death. Then someone referred me to Katie's teaching, and it ministered to me very deeply. I was blown away at the depth of her revelation regarding healing emotional wounds. That's why I am excited about this book.

Healing the Wounded Soul contains the road map that God used to heal my emotional wounds and restore my physical body. Like Katie's, my past was filled with darkness and drug addiction. Since coming out of that, I have dedicated my life to helping people overcome the things Satan has tried to use to defeat them.

I first pursued inner healing years ago. As a youth I suffered from extreme emotional and sexual abuse. I went to therapy and cried and cried at church altars for years. The pain inside me was so great that it actually felt like a knife in my heart. I tried counseling, deliverance prayer—nearly everything—but I still ached inside. People told me to just get over it, but as hard as I tried, I could not.

While the prayer and counseling helped to a certain degree, I experienced only minimal healing. When things got difficult,

I often reverted back to drinking, taking drugs, working excessively, or shutting down emotionally to deal with the pain. During this time in my life I found that many of the popular therapy and healing methods had their merits but often took years, if not decades, to bring freedom, and some people never broke free. Don't get me wrong. I think we need therapists and counselors. But I needed more, so I began crying out to the Lord to move mightily and bring healing to my soul and the souls of others.

MY BREAKTHROUGH

In 1992 I was reading the account in John 20 of Mary Magdalene visiting Jesus's tomb after He had been crucified and buried. When I read that, for the first time I saw how Jesus dealt with emotional wounds. There are a lot of examples of physical healing in the Bible, but until that day I had not seen how Jesus dealt with the emotional wounds in a person's soul.

When Mary arrived at the tomb, the stone covering the entrance had been rolled aside. She knelt down and looked within, only to find that Jesus's body was not there. She began crying because she felt a profound loss, not realizing that Jesus had been resurrected from the dead.

Jesus then appeared behind Mary as she was weeping and looking into the tomb, but she did not recognize Him at first. Jesus knew that Mary's feelings of grief and loss were because of what was in that tomb. But He called her away from it and spoke to her in a way that opened her eyes. The lesson here is that when God does something new in our lives, it might look different than we expect and may require a 180-degree turnaround.

I also had a revelation regarding the two angels inside the

tomb. God showed me that He places angels and help inside our pain and losses and that we will find them if we look for them. As I invited Jesus and His angels into the tombs of my losses and pain, I started getting major healing and my recovery came quickly. After trying to get healed for years, I was soon able to move beyond my pain and start helping others.

Years Later

After following Jesus for more than twenty-five years and being in full-time ministry, I found myself once again experiencing affliction in my mind. I had lost many of my family members to a devastating and fatal genetic disorder called Huntington's disease. I was diagnosed with it in 2001, and there is no cure or remission for this horrific sickness that wipes out families.

More than fifteen years ago God performed an amazing miracle in my life, and I was healed of all symptoms of Huntington's. At age fifty-eight I am still symptom-free, which is unheard of in the medical community. I am being placed in a special study because my physicians consider this an "anomaly," which is doctor-speak for a miracle!

Unfortunately I lost my mom, aunt, three uncles, and a first cousin to Huntington's—all in the same year. Since then I have lost several others, including my sister and brother. My mother and aunt were two of the most faith-filled believers I knew. To see them suddenly taken out and dying in their early sixties was traumatic for me.

Then I had to start caring for my oldest sister, who had helped raise me. She died a very slow, painful death at a young age. I spent years visiting hospitals and hospice care centers as I watched those I loved die no matter how hard I prayed, fasted, and worshipped over them.

Even though I was healed, I have not seen anyone else in

my family receive this same miracle. As a result my soul was wounded once again.

MY SOUL WOUNDS

In 2010 my oldest sister, Glenna, was getting sicker and I had to force her into nursing care for her own safety. At the time, I was traveling and doing ministry in churches and conferences around the world. I was accustomed to seeing God move and perform miracles in people's lives. It broke my heart to see Glenna in this condition. She was a strong believer, and we would always laugh together during our difficult times growing up.

I did not immediately realize it, but in 2013 I started to slowly decline in my health. I was becoming depressed, though I never would have admitted it, being the positive prophetic minister and believer that I am. I use prophetic, anointed stand-up comedy as part of my ministry because of my outlook. Laughter is medicine to the soul, but this funny guy was going through a major crisis. I was stricken with grief watching yet another family member die before me. I understood in my head that it was not from God, but I was carrying wounds in my heart and soul.

MEETING KATIE

When I met Katie Souza, it was my first interaction with someone who carried the same revelation I had received of Jesus healing the tombs of our past. I knew the blood of Jesus covered our sins but discovered that the *dunamis* power of Jesus healed our souls. Katie's revelation and understanding of God's ministry to our wounded souls is beyond anything I have ever seen or experienced.

I began to clean out the tombs of my past and invite dunamis into them. I have to say, I have received more healing through Katie's ministry in the last year than I have experienced my entire life. When I applied the lessons from her teachings to my life, I received deep healing and have seen miracles. I am now restored back to my calling.

As you read this book, expect to receive abundantly and enter to a place with the Lord that you have never been before!

—Doug Addison
InLight Connection
DOUGADDISON.COM

Chapter 1

WHY I COULDN'T CHANGE

I COULDN'T UNDERSTAND WHAT on earth made me act the way I did. I wasn't beaten or abandoned as a child. My family wasn't poor or destitute. In fact, we lived quite well, and I had a good relationship with both my parents. My mom was the perfect combination of tough and loving. She took me fishing and taught me how to shoot, yet she was also there when I was hurt and needed her comfort. My dad was often gone on business trips, but we knew he loved us. He never laid a hand on me or my sister except to spank me once, which I unquestionably deserved.

So why was I so out of control? Well, for one, I was addicted to the meth I cooked. My stuff was good, so I would stay up for days at a time tweaking[1] while executing as much chaos as possible. I later learned the real reason behind all my destructive behaviors, but before I did, I took down not only myself but also many of those around me.

Meth fueled my already massive anger problem, so I lived in a constant state of over-the-top rage, which assisted me in my other occupation as a "collector." When people owed me or someone else money, I would go get it—for a commission, of course. If the debtors didn't want to give it up, I would take it by force.

Collecting was my one "joy" in life. I liked terrorizing and hurting others—especially "bad" people. I didn't go after the nice folks. I never hurt or robbed someone who didn't deserve it. I went after only those who had taken something that wasn't theirs or injured people who couldn't stick up for themselves. I hated those types with a passion. Unfortunately I found that some of the world's biggest, meanest dudes were in that category, and though I thoroughly enjoyed going head-to-head with them, my bravado nearly cost me my life.

My violent disposition caused me to be arrested twelve times in one year. I was finally apprehended by a federal marshal and given a twelve-and-a-half-year prison sentence. But the last four months I lived on the streets before my arrest were the climax of a lifestyle of fury that almost got me killed.

RETRIEVING A FRIEND'S STOLEN GOODS

I hung my head out the passenger side of the truck I was riding in, my long hair blowing violently in the wind as we sped down the highway. We were part of a small convoy of two vehicles. Ours was in the front, leading the way. A mechanic friend of mine was driving, and a biker named Big Jim was sitting next to me. The stereo was blasting out AC/DC's "Back in Black," and we were all violently head banging along with the song. I was getting psyched up on purpose. This was not just a regular joy ride; I was packing (a gun), which meant we were on our way to do a job.

I had just made a new friend named Sammy. She was a drug dealer, and I was introduced to her when she needed to buy meth from a source who had really good dope. Mine was high-grade crystal, and when I gave her a sample, she was immediately interested.

Sammy was extraordinarily nice, and my heart felt for her because she had to sell dope to pay her bills. The more we hung out, the more I learned about her life. So when she told me the story of a certain biker dude who had ripped her off, I found myself quite irritated. They had cut a business deal. She had given him a bunch of household merchandise, and he had agreed to sell it for a commission. But after she handed it over, she never heard from him again.

Her story fit my narrative perfectly: poor, helpless girl gets taken by big, mean biker dude. This was a situation that was right up my alley. Immediately I offered to take care of it for her. She gladly accepted.

I had heard of this guy before. He was enormous and had a reputation for being extremely fierce. "All the better," I thought. "I will show him that he needs to pick on someone his own size—namely me." I don't recall his real name now, but at the time I called him "the monster."

Foolishly I never considered I would get hurt doing collections because I was just plain "psycho" in those days. My anger and rage were so intense they fueled me and made me feel like Superwoman, bulletproof and invincible.

So there we were, my friends and I, roaring off to do a collection on this guy. Sammy was in the vehicle behind us. When we arrived at the monster's place, I knocked on the door and discovered he wasn't home.

Suddenly he pulled up in his truck and came to a stop in the front yard. Big Jim and I strolled over to meet him. He stepped out, came toward us with a menacing walk, and stopped just inches from me. Looming over me with his huge frame, he stared me in the eye and said with a growl, "What do you want?"

Craning my neck as far back as it could go, I stared up at him and asked, "Do you know a girl named Sammy?"

He said, "Who?"

I repeated, "Sammy. You have a bunch of her stuff, and you owe her money. I came to get what is hers."

His eyes turned into slits as he glared at me and said, "I don't know who you're talking about."

I said, "You don't know who I am talking about?"

He repeated, "That's right. I don't know who you're talking about."

It was a lame attempt to deny the truth. Figuring he needed a little help to "remember," I reached behind my back, pulled my pistol out from my waistband, and shoved it in his face, all in one fast move. "Do you know who I am talking about now, man?" I asked in a low, threatening tone.

His countenance changed instantly. He turned from a monster into a sniveling little girl. I screamed, "Get in the house!" And he scrambled off, with us right on his tail.

A group of people were inside. When we walked in with the gun pulled, all conversation stopped. They knew something serious was going down. Looking at me in shock, the ones who knew me started muttering among themselves, "What is she doing here?" The ones who didn't were asking the others who I was. I heard snippets of stories of my violent history being quickly shared among them.

I looked at the group and said, "Well, now that you've got it all figured out, everybody stay right where you are." I quickly walked back to the front door, opened it, and signaled for the passengers in our other vehicle to come in, including Sammy.

When she entered the house, I turned to the monster and said, "Do you recognize this woman?" He blurted out, "Oh, yeah. Hey, Sammy! How you doing?" His tone was completely different. I shook my head in disgust. It always amazed me how much people changed when a gun was brought into the picture.

"I'm glad we got that straightened out. Now where is her stuff?" I demanded.

"It's not too far from here," he said, "right down the street in my storage." He was being so compliant I didn't have to threaten him anymore to get information.

"Well, guess what?" I said with a big smile on my face. "You're going to take us there right now!"

And out the door we went. In less than five minutes we were at his storage facility. The monster rolled up two doors, revealing an enormous stash of goodies, including Sammy's stuff. It was a treasure house. I told him he had to return all her items plus anything else she wanted.

"It's an interest payment," I said, "for you having her property for so long." He sadly nodded his head as he walked away to execute the tasks. But before he could go, I stopped him again. "And one more thing," I added with a big smile, "I get to pick whatever I want too." He paused, and I saw him tense up a little bit. "It's my commission. I know you don't mind, right?" He didn't argue but nodded his head in resignation and let me shop at my own convenience.

It was a good day but only the beginning of my bucket list. I had many irons in the fire that needed to be dealt with. Each one presented a new and dangerous situation that brought me close to death because unfortunately things weren't going to go my way anymore.

One incident in particular signaled the beginning of the end.

LOSING MY HOME

I had just met a new guy whom I'll call Lincoln. I was hanging out with an acquaintance named Lana, and she had some friends who needed help with a collection. When I offered, she said her friend Lincoln was already on it. Intrigued, I asked if I could ride along during the job. She agreed, so we drove down to meet him at the house of the people who owed the money.

We were parked around the corner when Lincoln pulled up. Instantly I knew we were in for a good time. He was driving a souped-up truck that he had rigged to crush cars. Lincoln used it to punish people who didn't comply with their collections. Nothing persuades a person to pay his bill more than the thought of his car being folded in half!

We drove to the house only to discover no one was home. Just as Lincoln was turning around to go back, we heard the roar of a Firebird coming around the corner. It was the people we were looking for. When they saw Lincoln's truck, they slammed on the brakes and threw their car in reverse, the tires squealing as they backed at high speed down the street. Lincoln took off in hot pursuit, and his truck caught up with their car, driving them into a ditch, but they punched their way out and sped down the road onto the freeway.

The chase that ensued was right out of the movies. Lana was covering her eyes, screaming, while I was yelling and cheering Lincoln on. I had barely met this guy but knew we were cut from the same cloth. We lost our prey that night, but the evening wasn't a total bust, as I had met a new friend, one who would soon become my greatest adversary.

Months went by, and Lincoln and I got tight. I felt I had finally met someone who not only could keep up with me but also surpassed me in psychotic behavior. Then I made a fatal mistake. I fed him too much good dope, and he spun out of control and lost it on me.

One night I went to hang out with a high-level dealer. Lincoln wasn't happy about it. When I returned, I discovered he had used his truck to maul the car I had parked at Lana's. Not only that, but when I went down to the place where I had stashed the RV that I cooked dope in and lived in, the RV was gone. Lincoln was one of the few people who knew where it was.

Lincoln was an expert at both hunting people and hiding things. It took me a month to find the RV. When I did, I borrowed a big truck from a friend and took a guy named Marcos with me to get it. When I came to a stop on the road outside where it was being stashed, I told Marcos to wait until I drove the RV away before he left. But before I could get out of the truck, I noticed in my rearview mirror a foreign sports car coming up the road behind me. I didn't think anything of it until I saw an AR-15 assault rifle hanging out the driver's side window.

"Lincoln," I said with disgust. The driver holding the AR-15 stuck his body sideways out the window, looking like a rooster cocking his head. Then the passenger door opened, and out came Lincoln, sauntering up to my window.

"I came to get my RV," I announced.

He said nothing but suddenly cocked his fist back and hit me on the side of the face with a fierce right hook. My head snapped sideways; then I slowly turned back to look at him and said, "You hit like a girl." I was shocked that he didn't clock me again. Instead, he quickly headed back to his car. I knew he was going for his weapon.

I was outgunned, so I did the only thing I could. I threw the truck into drive and punched it. The street we were on was a winding back road that was very narrow. It was just like the mountain road in Hawaii that I had driven every day to school when I was growing up. Muscle memory kicked in, and I flew down that road as if I had wings instead of wheels. I quickly outdistanced the sports car, whose driver obviously didn't have the skill to handle the amazing machine that was under him.

I completely lost them when I hit the highway that intersected the street I was on. Without slowing down, I flew out into the afternoon traffic like a cork coming out of a champagne bottle. Luck and skill enabled me to slide into a small hole in the fast-moving traffic. As the truck took a hard bounce into the lane, Marcos screamed, "Whoa, girl, you know how to drive!" I ignored his compliment. I was too focused on saving our lives.

Then I looked in the rearview mirror. The guy driving the sports car had zero guts. He had come to a full stop at the intersection I had just rocked through. I was putting real distance between him and us. At the next major intersection I jetted out into the opposite lane and took a left, cutting over the sidewalk. At that point he was nowhere in sight.

Marcos and I hid until dark, and then I drove back to where the RV was parked so I could get it. It was gone, of course, because I was dealing with no ordinary person; I was fighting against the mirror image of myself.

It took me another month to find out that Lincoln had sold the RV to a guy who lived in a literal fortress—a junkyard surrounded by a huge fence with a massive metal gate. I went down there with one of my closet friends and waited on the side of the property. As soon as someone pulled up and the gate opened, I jumped out and forced everyone in the car inside at gunpoint. When I walked into the RV my heart sank. All the expensive equipment I had owned, plus the cool décor, was gone, replaced by a bunch of tweeker junk.

I turned around, looked at the people who ran the place, and told them to get their stuff out. They were so afraid they didn't even bother arguing with me about the fact that they had paid money for the RV I was now taking from them. Instead, they quickly obeyed and scrambled to grab their belongings. But I drove out of there no happier than I was when I went in. Even though I got my house back, I was totally enraged and wanted justice.

A month later things had gotten so bad I decided to leave town. I packed up every treasure I had in the RV and took off. At the very outskirts of the city the vehicle broke down. I hid it behind a skating rink and went to find a mechanic friend of mine to fix the problem. When we returned, the parking lot was full of fire trucks because the RV was going up in flames. Surprisingly it was not Lincoln who set fire to it but another guy I was warring with. I had taken his fancy sports car at gunpoint from a friend of his whom he let drive it. Burning the RV was his retaliation.

I immediately responded by going to his house and taking his beloved truck. But it wasn't enough. The RV incident pushed me over the edge. I had almost made it out. Now here I was with nothing left, dangling at the end of my rope. I soon discovered that when you're in that place, you make some very unwise decisions. Little did I know mine would come close to doing me in.

A COLLECTION GONE BAD

I decided to collect on every single person who owed me and to take whatever I wanted just because I could. Unfortunately I was owed by a bunch of stone-cold killers. One person especially would almost be the end of me.

My association with Mason was amicable at first. I actually liked hanging out at the clubhouse where he spent most of his time. It was on a large property at the edge of town that was totally fenced in and protected by vicious animals.

We did business, got high together, and had some good laughs. But one bad deal led to another until I was owed and angry about it. He had a classic truck of mine that he said had been "mistakenly" cut up. I loved that truck and was really upset when I heard what had happened to it. I kept pushing him and his fellow bikers to make good on my loss, but they never did. Because of all the other stuff that had been going on in my life, I was out of patience. I was ready to go to war over this situation and didn't care what the consequences would be.

Done with their stalling, I went over to the clubhouse one night with a buddy. There was a long driveway outside the fence, leading to the property, and cars were lined up along the entire thing. My friend and I parked at the very back, and I told him to leave if he heard shooting. I walked down the driveway past all the cars and jumped the gate. Looking out for the animals, I made it to the front door unscathed.

When Mason opened it, he didn't look pleased. He knew what I was there for: payment. He reluctantly let me in, and I discovered why there were so many cars outside. The house was full of guests because a representative from one of the biggest biker clubs was there to induct Mason into the club. They had brought him a vest with their colors and planned to give it to him that night. It was considered a huge honor. All the members were there to celebrate.

When Mason introduced me to the main man—the representative of the club—I could tell by the look on his face that he had heard of me and was not happy I was there. I sat down in a chair across from him, and he immediately tried to intimidate me. He pulled out his knife and a sharpening stone and proceeded to run the blade back and forth over the stone while staring at me. The more he did it, the more I smiled, until finally I tilted my head to the right, exposing my neck to him, and pointing, I said, "Right here, that's a good place to stick it."

He couldn't hide his shock. He didn't think anyone would have the guts to challenge him—especially a girl. The air thickened and the place got quiet as the other guests picked up on our exchange. I thought, "This is it. You really stepped over the line this time, Kate." But I didn't care. I was totally done. All I saw in front of me was a puffed-up pile of dirt that was sucking up air. What made him think he was any better than I was and that I should be afraid of him?

Just when I thought he was going to lunge at my throat, Mason came into the room and signaled for me to come and talk with him privately. His entrance probably saved me—for the moment, at least. The rep from the club and I broke eye contact, and I got up to follow my onetime friend out of the room.

Once we were in his bedroom, Mason started arguing and giving his reasons for not paying up. As the conversation got very heated, I saw him glance over at the bed. The butt of a .45-caliber pistol was sticking out from under a pile of clothes. Suddenly it was as if we could read each other's mind. Who could get to it first? The tension grew as that thought started to become a reality. Suddenly the door to the room opened.

It was the rep from the club. He walked in with the vest, showing it in an attempt to frighten me. He was trying to tell me that to mess with Mason was to mess with all of them. I wasn't impressed even though I guess I should have been. I told Mason I would talk to him again when we wouldn't be bothered, and I left. I later found out that the rep ordered a hit on me and intended to fulfill it himself. However, he never got the chance because he was killed in a motorcycle accident shortly afterward.

The events of that night pushed Mason over the edge. I don't think he could forgive me for daring to stand up to him and his friend in front of their guests. So from that moment on he plotted to kill me—and almost succeeded.

THE END OF STREET LIFE

One day Mason called me requesting a truce. He wanted to meet and promised he would give me everything I was owed. I knew taking his offer might be a deadly mistake, but I needed funds badly. I soon found out that he was nicknamed Killer for a reason.

We agreed to meet at a public restaurant, and he told me PeeWee would be coming with him. PeeWee's appearance was the exact opposite of his name. He was tall and very round. I went alone because I didn't know a single person who had the guts to go head-to-head with these guys.

Sitting at the table with them was weird. They were both very friendly—too friendly. I was promised everything I wanted and more. It all seemed too good to be true. I knew they were up to something.

We decided to leave and go to their shop. Mason gave me a tour of the place, showing me some bike parts and even a couple of Harley-Davidson basket cases. At the end of the tour he promised to give me a truck that he had parked in the back. It wasn't enough, but it was a good start.

Suddenly I noticed that PeeWee had slipped away while I was distracted with the conversation.

"Hey, where's PeeWee?" I asked, trying to sound nonchalant.

"Oh, he had to go take care of something," Mason replied. Then he did something very stupid. He flashed me a big, phony smile. It was time to leave. Something was going down. I quickly wrapped up the details about when to pick up my prizes, and we both walked outside to our vehicles. He got in his truck, and I jumped on the stolen motorcycle I had ridden in on.

He yelled out the window, "Meet me at the clubhouse if you want some money."

"Yeah, right," I thought. "Over my dead body." At the time, I did not realize how much truth was in that thought.

The shop was on a one-way street that turned into a tight figure eight as it met the ramp to the freeway. I turned right on it and punched the bike hard. Within a few seconds I hit fifty-five, but then suddenly the chain of my bike snapped and wrapped around the back tire, sending me into a straight skid.

Instantly I realized where PeeWee went when he disappeared. He had gone outside and done something to the bike.

Within seconds I T-boned a curb, and the bike popped straight up in the air, flipped end over end three times, and sent me flying. I came down hard on my head, bounced, and skidded across the asphalt. Soon a security guard came running toward me while calling the police. I tried to stop him, saying, "No, no, don't do that. I'm fine. I've got it." But when I tried to pick up the bike, I couldn't. Later on I discovered I had a broken collarbone.

I looked down and saw pieces of my flesh hanging off my hands. Then I heard the guard behind me on his walkie-talkie calling for the cops and an ambulance. I started walking away very fast, leaving the bike behind. I looked ahead and realized the only place I could flee to was the shop with the men who had just tried to kill me!

FINDING GOD IN THE DARKNESS

As I limped quickly toward the huge shop doors, Mason's men tried to close them before I could get there. I was only a few feet away when cops turned onto the corner of the street and hit the siren. As they did, the sound of it sent a shock wave through my body, and pure adrenaline sent me leaping through the doors a second before they closed behind me.

I had jumped out of the frying pan into the fire. The guys

who had just tried to take my life surrounded me. No one said a word. I growled, "The cops are outside, but not for long. They will be in here soon." Thankfully they realized it was not a good time to finish me off lest their involvement become known.

As I predicted, it didn't take the cops long to find out the bike was stolen, and they initiated an all-out search for me. Police helicopters came and, using their spotlights, searched for me for hours while I hid under a desk in the deepest parts of the shop.

Bleeding and torn up, I was extremely dizzy from the massive head trauma I had received. I couldn't even move without spinning, so I stayed hunkered down until the helicopters finally left. Barely able to stand, I crawled out from under the desk and went into a bathroom to clean up. Slowly and painfully I stripped off my leathers and washed myself as best I could. Blood, asphalt, and dirt had dried on my cheeks, hair, and hands. My broken collarbone made every movement excruciating and nearly impossible.

When I peeled back my jeans, I found a huge swollen place on my hip, and in the middle of it was a five-inch blood clot with torn flesh on the surface. As I gingerly inspected it, I could feel loose bone fragments floating around under the skin. Not good.

To avoid any more police entanglements, I needed to look different when I walked out. So after I cleaned up, I slicked back my long hair into a ponytail and kept the leathers folded over my arm. Then I calmly walked out of the shop past my adversaries. They stared me down but let me go. I made it out of there alive but not well. I was hurt badly but couldn't go to the hospital for fear of being arrested. I'd just have to let the wounds heal on their own.

I was in such bad shape that I was unable to even muscle

anyone for cash or get the supplies I desperately needed to cook a batch of meth. But I had to get money fast. That's when two very resourceful guys I knew from the streets tried to talk me into cooking a batch of dope with them. I never took in partners because I reasoned that no one could rat on you if you worked alone. But they continued to push, claiming they could get all the supplies I needed and provide a house in which I could cook in exchange for my giving them a percentage of the finished product. For weeks I fiercely declined their offer, until I couldn't hold out anymore. So I went with them and quickly discovered I made the biggest mistake of my life. I found out later that the house they took me to was already known by the cops as a meth lab. Within twenty-four hours of going up to the place, I was sitting handcuffed in the back of a federal marshal's car.

After my trial I was sentenced to twelve and a half years in prison. Oddly enough, once I was behind bars, God wasted no time getting hold of me. The only book inside my unit was a Bible, and I threw myself into reading it. Fascinated, I couldn't get enough. It was the coolest thing I had ever read. Soon I used my "leadership" qualities to bring almost everyone in my unit to Christ.

A NEED FOR HEALING

However, there was a big problem. Even though I was born again, I was still acting like the old Kate. Not a week went by without my fighting with someone, getting written up, or attacking a police officer. What in the world was wrong? The Bible told me I was now a "new creation" in Christ. Why wasn't I acting like one? I was just as violent and rebellious as ever, though I sincerely loved God and wanted to please Him.

Month after month I was repeatedly sent to lockdown for

my latest infraction. Each time, I pondered why I couldn't stop doing what I was doing—what I had always done in the face of something I didn't like. Finally the Holy Spirit began to reveal to me the answer I was searching for: though my spirit man had been made perfect when I gave my life to Christ, my soul was still unregenerate. It was wounded and desperately needed healing.

Over time God taught me how the soul becomes wounded, what the effects of that wounding are, and how to apply His remedies so that I—and all believers who receive this revelation—can walk in the fullness of the freedom Christ died to give us. That is what this book is about. Christ didn't offer up His life just so you could be saved and spend eternity with Him in heaven but also so you could be healed and live on Earth in true peace, joy, and happiness. I want to show you how.

Prayer Activation

If you are not saved—in other words, if you have never given your life to Christ and received Him as your Savior—begin by praying this prayer:

> Lord Jesus, I know that I am a sinner. I have done things that are not pleasing to You, and I repent of them now. Please forgive me and come to live in my heart. I receive You as my Lord and Savior and commit my life to You. Thank You for hearing and answering my prayer. Amen.

Afterward pray:

Lord Jesus, I purpose to love You with my whole heart, mind, soul, and strength and to obey Your Word. But I know I can't do those things successfully while my soul is wounded. Please help me to understand what that means through studying the revelation in this book and to find healing by applying the remedies You have already provided.

Chapter 2

THE WOUNDED SOUL

I T'S IMPORTANT TO understand what it means to have a wounded soul and how it can affect, control, and devastate every area of your life. I believe you will be surprised at how many problematic issues you deal with that have as their source your unhealed inner man. Once you start receiving soul healing through the power of Jesus's sacrifice and resurrection, you will walk in a realm of supernatural power and provision that you have not experienced before! But first you must know something about the way God designed human beings.

WE ARE MADE UP OF THREE PARTS

You may be surprised to learn that God created you as a three-part being. All you can see is your body, but you also have a spirit and a soul housed in that body. First Thessalonians 5:23 makes it very clear that God created you this way.

> Now may the God of peace Himself sanctify you completely; and may your whole spirit, soul, and body be preserved blameless at the coming of our Lord Jesus Christ.

According to this verse, it's God's will to sanctify and make blameless every part of who you are—body, soul, and spirit. Some people don't believe this is possible because we constantly think wrong thoughts, feel hurtful emotions, and become weak and sick. However, we can't base our doctrine on personal experiences. Rather, we must believe the truth of Scripture. There are many places in the Word that prove that God's will for us is to be whole in every part of our beings and that He has provided the power we need to make this happen.

PERFECTED IN SPIRIT

When you received Jesus Christ into your life, your spirit was made instantly complete. The Bible says the same Spirit that lives in Christ now lives in you (Col. 1:27). Because Christ is perfect, your spirit man is also flawless. It never sins, never gets upset, and always trusts God. Your spirit has been made brand-new. This is why the Bible says, "Therefore, if anyone is in Christ, he is a new creation; old things have passed away; behold, all things have become new" (2 Cor. 5:17).

When I first read that verse, I thought, "If I am a totally new creation, how come I feel like a wreck and am acting worse?" The answer is because when a person is born again, only one part of him is perfected. The rest is not. His body and his soul—which is made up of his mind, will, and emotions—still need healing.

THE NEED TO BE TRANSFORMED

Romans 12:2 says, "And do not be conformed to this world [any longer with its superficial values and customs], but be transformed and progressively changed [as you mature spiritually] by the renewing of your mind [focusing on godly values and ethical attitudes], so that you may prove [for yourselves] what the will of God is, that which is good and acceptable and perfect [in His plan and purpose for you]" (AMP).

This scripture commands you to be transformed in your mind, which is part of your soul. The word *transformed* (*metamorphoó*) means "the change of moral character for the better."[1] Once you're born again, your spirit man has perfect morals. It never acts stupid. In fact, the Bible says you are the righteousness of God in Christ. But your soul, which includes your mind, needs to be renewed and changed so that it can actually walk in the righteousness that has been won for you.

Notice that Romans 12:2 says your soul transformation happens "progressively." That means the healing of your mind and your inner man doesn't take place instantly when you get saved. Rather, as you will soon see, it unfolds step-by-step as you apply the power and presence of Jesus Christ that you are going to learn about in this study.

Being transformed in your mind and the other parts of your soul will cause you to experience massive breakthrough. As Romans 12:2 indicates, it will give you the ability to discern the good and perfect will of God for your life. Think about that. If you're always in the middle of God's will, then you will experience success and victory in every situation you deal with. Being changed and healed in your mind, will, and emotions causes this to happen.

The reason your soul needs healing is because we are all wounded. This is not hard to believe, as life presents endless challenges, trials, and persecutions that can leave scars on our inner man. No one is exempt. In fact, all of mankind feels the pain and pressure inside themselves of the daily assaults we are under. Sometimes these burdens of the soul can be so momentous they drive people to totally give up. That's how much power soul wounds have. They are able to devastate us and wipe out our hope and even life itself. Therefore we must be diligent to pursue what Jesus has supplied for us—the power of soul healing.

You may be wondering *how* our souls get wounded. I believe there are three main things that wound the soul: sin, trauma, and generational iniquities. Let's look at them.

SIN WOUNDS THE SOUL

Two types of sin can wound us and put us in need of healing.

Sins we commit

Many of the wounds in our souls are created by sins we commit—adultery, fornication, gossiping, drinking or eating to excess, idolatry, emotional outbursts, wrong thinking, taking offense, and so on. Sin of any kind can wound you. In fact, all sins, especially if they are habitual, have the potential to injure your soul.

Isaiah 30:26 says, "The Lord binds up the hurt of His people, and heals their wound [inflicted by Him because of their sins]" (AMPC). According to this scripture, wounds can be formed in you through sin. The word "wound" is the Hebrew word *sheber*, which can mean "breaches and wounds," including wounds "of the mind."[2] Sin can literally wound every part of your soul, including your mind.

Do you remember the story in the Bible that tells how King David committed adultery with Bathsheba and then arranged for her husband, Uriah the Hittite, to be killed in battle in order to cover it up? (See 2 Samuel 11:1–4; 14–17.) In Psalm 38:5 David tells us the consequences of his sin: "My wounds fester and are loathsome because of my sinful folly" (NIV).

According to David, his sins literally wounded him. In fact, he experienced such extreme soul pain from those wounds that he said they were festering and loathsome.

Once your inner man is wounded by sin, it needs to be healed just as your body needs to be healed when it gets sick.

Psalm 41:4 says, "Lᴏʀᴅ, be merciful unto me: heal my soul; for I have sinned against thee" (ᴋᴊᴠ).

The psalmist clearly understood two things: (1) sin can wound the soul, and (2) once it does, your inner man needs healing. Through this book you will learn how to wipe out the sin that has wounded you and then heal your soul so that you can truly experience the abundance of life Jesus came to give you.

Sins committed against you

Your soul can also become wounded when someone sins against you. Have you ever been talked about, mentally or physically abused, neglected, or rejected? Throughout the ages fallen man has proved over and over how quick we are to attack, assault, and devastate those around us.

First Corinthians 8:12 says, "But when you thus sin against the brethren, and wound their weak conscience, you sin against Christ." The word *conscience* here means "the soul."[3] When you sin against someone or someone sins against you, the result is that the soul gets wounded. As you will see, there are many consequences that come from a soul wound, including getting sick in one's mind and emotions and even becoming physically ill.

One of the biggest ways people hurt one another is through their words. Proverbs 26:22 reveals how gossip and slander can cause injury: "The words of a whisperer or slanderer are like dainty morsels or words of sport [to some, but to others are like deadly wounds]; and they go down into the innermost parts of the body [or of the victim's nature]" (ᴀᴍᴘᴄ).

According to this verse, slanderous words create "deadly wounds" in a person's innermost being. When you whisper words of gossip or speak evil against someone, it can create such hurt and pain in his soul that the wounds become a threat to his very existence.

Unfortunately the people you talk about aren't the only ones who suffer. Your negative words can become deadly wounds to yourself! Gossip is addictive, and human beings naturally like to complain about difficult people and situations in their lives. However, what you don't realize is that when you talk smack, not only is the person you're speaking about hurt; it also causes deadly wounds to form in your own soul!

I was ministering in a prison once. While in the chaplain's office I was getting words of knowledge for the female inmates gathered there. At one point I looked at a woman standing in front of me and heard the Lord say she had a rotten, painful tooth. When I asked her if it was true, she said yes. Then I heard the word *property*. Inmates' belongings are often called their "property" and are kept in a property box. As I heard the word, I got the feeling that someone had messed with her belongings. When I inquired, she confirmed that a corrections officer had gone into her property box and taken something that belonged to her. Then she looked at me with a flare of anger in her eyes and said, "And I wasn't OK with it."

I asked if she responded by speaking evil words against that officer. She admitted that she had. So I explained Proverbs 26:22 to her and led her through repentance for the slanderous words she had spoken, which became deadly wounds to the officer's soul and hers. After that I prayed for her soul to be healed and commanded the rot in her tooth to be removed, the pain to leave, and new enamel to grow. When I asked her how the aching in her tooth was, she looked up at me with wide eyes and said, smiling, "It's gone!" Then I went back out to the meeting, where a hundred or so female inmates were gathered. I asked how many of them had pain or problems with their teeth. Dozens of them raised their hands. After I explained Proverbs 26:22, I asked how many of them had been speaking evil about a corrections officer or another person. Practically the whole room raised their hands. So I led them through repentance and commanded their souls to be healed of the deadly wounds they created with their negative words. Then I commanded bacteria in their teeth to die, pain to leave, and new enamel to grow. When I asked how many felt the pain leave and something shift in their mouths, almost all of them raised their hands.

Bottom line: stop talking about people if you don't want to be wounded and get sick!

TRAUMA WOUNDS THE SOUL

This world is a traumatic place to live. Every day I hear horror stories from people around the globe describing devastating situations in their relationships, finances, or other areas. But here is the worst thing about trauma: it is so deadly that it can wound your soul and then destroy the rest of your life.

Do you remember what happened to Job, whose story is described in the book of the Bible named after him? He experienced some horrible traumas. On his eldest son's birthday, while his children were celebrating, the Sabeans stole all his oxen and donkeys and slew all his servants. Then fire fell from heaven and burned up all his sheep and the servants who were tending them. Then the Chaldeans stole his vast herds of camels. After that a great whirlwind came and destroyed the house his children were celebrating in and killed them all. If that wasn't enough, Satan came and smote Job with painful boils from his head to his feet. (See Job 1:13–19; 2:7.)

That is a lot of trauma for one man to endure! What effect did these painful events have on Job's life? They wounded his soul. We know this is true because Job himself declared, "I am weary of my life and loathe it! I will give free expression to my complaint; I will speak in the bitterness of my soul" (Job 10:1, AMPC).

Here Job expresses how bitter he was feeling in his soul because of the excruciating traumas he had lived through. In fact, twenty-three times he describes the pain he was feeling in his inner man because of the horrors he had experienced. He described his soul as being "vexed" (Job 27:2, KJV) and "poured out" (Job 30:16).

Everyone on earth has lived through a devastating trauma of some kind, if not many of them. Sometimes I think Satan engineers difficult circumstances just so he can keep us wounded.

Because trauma is so prevalent in our everyday lives, we must watch over our souls to make sure we stay healthy in the midst of every trying situation. I can't tell you how many hundreds and thousands of physical miracles I have seen after people got healed of the trauma of a divorce, a car accident, a death in the family, or the loss of their children. I have seen bones grow, diseases leave, and pain totally disappear when people's souls were healed of the wounds they had received from a trauma they experienced.

Here's a good example: A woman in one of my meetings had been in two car accidents over a period of years. In the first one, she broke her neck in two places and also numerous parts of her spine. Her condition was so bad she was told she would never walk again. Just when she started to recover, she was in another crash. This time she broke her leg and her hip and could no longer bend her leg at all. This was especially troubling because it restricted a lot of her activities and because she liked to spend her prayer time sitting cross-legged on the floor.

During the meeting she cried as she sensed God healing her

soul from the ordeals she had endured. She realized she could bend her leg for the first time since the accident and that she had no pain. She even came up on stage and demonstrated her miracle by plopping down on the floor cross-legged!

A woman in another meeting also received a physical miracle when she was healed of the trauma of a car accident. During the accident she had hit her head and developed tinnitus. Every day for years she had ringing, roaring, buzzing, and sometimes pain in her ear. The night of the meeting I taught on trauma and spoke a word of knowledge about an ear being healed, and the noise in this woman's ear completely stopped! When the healing manifested, she didn't come up right away because she wanted to make sure she was really healed. But the next day, when there was still no sign of the tinnitus, she joyfully came up to testify of her miraculous healing.

Generational Iniquities Cause Soul Wounds

Soul wounds can be caused by generational iniquities. These are habitual sins committed by our ancestors that have not been repented of and forgiven and that are passed on to us while we are being formed in the womb. As God said to the Israelites: "I, the LORD your God, am a jealous God, visiting the iniquity of the fathers upon the children to the third and fourth generations of those who hate Me" (Deut. 5:9).

The word for womb in Greek is *koilia*. It refers to the place where a fetus is conceived and nurtured until birth, and it also means "the soul." [4] Why would the word *womb* also mean "soul"? Because when you were being knit together in your mother's womb, your inner man received all the sins and related wounds your ancestors had in their souls. David confirms this truth in Psalm 51:5: "Behold, I was shapen in iniquity; and in sin did my mother conceive me" (KJV).

The Bible uses many different words, such as *trespass* and *rebellion*, to describe sin. However, when it uses the word *iniquity*, it is referring to generational sins. David said that when he was in the womb, he was being "shapen in iniquity"; that is, he was receiving all the generational sins committed by the people in his bloodline. Since the Bible says that sin can wound the soul, then David was also receiving all the soul wounds created by his ancestors' sins.

David seemed to understand the wounded condition of his inner man because he then prayed, "Create in me a clean heart, O God; and renew a right spirit within me" (Ps. 51:10, KJV). The word "heart" in this verse is *leb* in Hebrew, which means "the soul." [5] After David declared that he had received all the sins and wounds in his bloodline while being formed in the womb, he then petitioned God to heal his soul of all the junk he was born with!

WOUNDS YOU ARE BORN WITH CAN MAKE YOU SICK

When soul wounds are inherited from our family line, they can cause disease to manifest in our bodies, as they did in the body of the lame man described in Acts 3:1–2 (KJV).

> Now Peter and John went up together into the temple at the hour of prayer, being the ninth hour. And a certain man lame from his mother's womb was carried, whom they laid daily at the gate of the temple which is called Beautiful, to ask alms of them that entered into the temple.

Notice this man was born with a physical sickness or disability that he got in the womb. Again, the word "womb" (*koilia*) means "the soul." So when he was being shaped in the womb he received a wound that was passed down to him through his family line, which caused him to be born lame.

When Peter was questioned by the rulers and elders about the healing, even Peter claimed the beggar's disease came from his soul. Peter answered them, "If we this day be examined of the good deed done to the impotent man, by what means he is made whole; be it known unto you all, and to all the people of Israel, that by the name of Jesus Christ of Nazareth, whom ye crucified, whom God raised from the dead, even by him doth this man stand here before you whole" (Acts 4:9–10, KJV).

Peter called the lame man "impotent." The Greek word translated "impotent" (*asthenēs*) means "strengthless."[6] It comes from a negative form of the root word *sthenoō*, which means "to make strong, to strengthen: one's soul."[7] The man's impotency in his body came about because he needed to be made strong in soul. Just as he was afflicted by the effects of generational iniquities, we can be too.

A woman who had developed a kidney problem as a result of a birth defect came to one of my meetings. For seven years her condition had caused her constant pain and prevented her from lying on a particular side. During worship she suddenly felt tingling and burning in her foot, and just like that the pain in her kidneys left. All my meetings are saturated with soul-healing power because that is what I carry. This woman was healed in her soul of a wound she received in the womb that caused her to be born with a physical defect. Once the wound was healed, she received a miracle.

One time I was speaking at a special meeting for women who were residents of halfway houses. The meeting was especially challenging because I had only thirty minutes to tell my testimony, do an altar call, and work miracles. Thankfully God came to the rescue and enabled me to get everything done in that short amount of time.

After I walked off the stage, a woman who was born with a birth defect that caused her to be blind in one eye was brought to me. Her condition was so rare that many doctors had a difficult time naming it. When they finally did, they were unable to give her any kind of treatment. Yet in that short meeting God went to work.

She started seeing during the healing activation. She explained that the eye had always been dark and that everything looked grey with no detail. Yet as she stood in front of me, she described what I looked like, including my hair color and style. God was healing her of a soul wound she received in the womb and the birth defect that was connected to it.

As you continue reading this study, you will be shocked at the wide variety of miracles people experience when their souls are healed. In the next chapter I will show you the effects that soul wounds—no matter whether they come from sin, trauma, or generational iniquities—can have on your life. Then I will teach you how to heal them so you can experience the impossible too.

Prayer Activation

Let's close this chapter with a prayer decree to get your soul healing started. Just read this out loud with me and believe that the Lord is going to immediately go to work.

> *Lord Jesus, I ask that You heal all the wounds in my soul. I believe that You can wash me clean of any sin that wounded me, heal me of every trauma I have lived through, and wipe out all the*

generational iniquities and wounds in my blood-line. I believe that You are the lover of my soul and will cause me to have breakthrough in every area where I need healing. I lift my praises to You and thank You in advance for the victory! In Jesus's name, amen.

Chapter 3

EFFECTS OF BEING WOUNDED

BEING AWARE OF the ways soul wounds can affect you is extremely important. If you don't know the root of a problem, how can you address it? But it's also important to realize that the list of effects in this chapter is in no way conclusive. The consequences of the wounded soul are so vast they can't be covered in just one book. Many more studies would need to be published to discuss even a fraction of their influence.

In later chapters I will cover some of the more serious effects of soul wounds—premature death, bone diseases, unusually high levels of demonic activity, food addictions, and weight gain—in more depth. But for now let's start with the basic issues that are the result of unhealed areas in your inner man.

SOUL WOUNDS CAN CAUSE YOU TO SIN

Wounds in your soul can control you and even drive you to sin. Read what the apostle Paul said in Romans 7:20 (AMPC):

> Now if I do what I do not desire to do, it is no longer I doing it [it is not myself that acts], but the sin [principle] which dwells within me [fixed and operating in my soul].

Paul said the last thing he desired to do was sin, but the junk in his soul literally overwhelmed him and made him do things he didn't want to do. What's in your soul can control you. The more wounded you are, the more of a mess you will be. My soul was so wounded that it caused me to do crazy things even after I was saved. If you're wounded, you too may find yourself doing things you don't want to do, such as getting offended easily or becoming depressed, bitter, anxious, fearful, and more.

There is only so much you can do in your own strength to control your behavior. You may be able to make yourself act right for a while, but it will be only a matter of time before you fall back into old patterns. You can hold your breath or swear up and down that you're not going to yell at your husband or your children. You can promise with all your heart that you will stop drinking, smoking, and talking about people. But eventually you will end up like Paul, doing things you don't want to do because of the sin principle that is fixed and operating in your soul! That's why you need to get your soul healed.

SOUL WOUNDS DETERMINE WHO YOU ARE AND WHAT YOU SAY

Proverbs 23:7 says that "as he thinks in his heart, so is he" (MEV). The word "heart" in this verse is the Hebrew word *nephesh*, which means "the soul."[1] Thus whatever is in your soul is who you are going to be. If there is pain and misery in there, then you will be a person who is constantly unhappy and unsatisfied. If fear rules your soul, you will be someone who walks around in constant dread. This is why it's vital to be healed in your inmost being. The more soul healing you get, the more you will become a totally different person and your life will be completely transformed.

I went from being a violent, bitter person to one of peace. If you are normally sad and depressed, then you will be a person of joy and happiness. When your soul is healed, you will become what is in your heart—a person filled and healed by the power of Jesus Christ!

The Bible also says "out of the abundance of the heart the mouth speaks" (Matt. 12:34, MEV). The word "heart" in this verse is the Greek word *kardia*, which means "the soul."[2] So this verse is saying that what's in your soul is what you're going to talk about. I can have a conversation with someone and in minutes tell how wounded she is by what and who she dialogues about.

Are you constantly complaining? Then there is an area in your soul that is not healed and causing you to walk in a spirit of discontentment. Do you often talk negatively about a certain person? Then something has happened between the two of you that caused you to be wounded, and now you are speaking out of those wounds.

Too often our mouths are the fountains that pour out the pain in our souls. Letting wounds direct your speech can be devastating to your life and health. The Bible says we can speak to a mountain, and it will be thrown into the sea (Mark 11:23). But if your words are constantly negative or faithless because of what you feel in your soul, then your words will have no power, and that mountain will stay right where it is.

SOUL WOUNDS NEGATIVELY CONTROL YOUR EMOTIONS

Are your emotions unbalanced and out of control? Do you find yourself constantly feeling fearful, anxious, angry, or depressed? Have you tried everything to stay calm and peaceful without results? It could be your unhealed soul that's affecting you.

Look at these revealing scriptures from Psalms that connect the condition of your emotions to your soul.

> They reward me evil for good, to the sorrow of my soul
> —PSALM 35:12

> Why are you cast down, O my soul? And why are you disquieted within me?
> —PSALM 42:5

> My soul refused to be comforted.
> —PSALM 77:2

> For my soul is full of troubles.
> —PSALM 88:3

> My soul melts from heaviness.
> —PSALM 119:28

Wow! According to these scriptures, it's your soul that causes you to feel sorrow, trouble, and heaviness. Being wounded may be the reason you refuse to be comforted in the midst of a trial or why your soul feels cast down and disquieted within you.

When you are healed, your emotions will change dramatically. You will be able to walk in balanced, healthy feelings, and your peace and joy levels will explode! Psalm 131:2 says, "Surely I have calmed and quieted my soul, like a weaned child with his mother; like a weaned child is my soul within me."

While a child is being weaned, he frets, fusses, squalls, and bawls. Ask yourself these questions:

- Am I always fretting, filled with worry, annoyed, and discontented?

- Do I fuss, complain, and argue with everyone about everything?

- During conflicts do I squall and bawl, even scream violently in the midst of the confrontation?

If so these are all signs that your soul is deeply wounded.

I should know because I was guilty of all of the above. I was always complaining and arguing with people, and screaming was the way I conducted my fights. I was such an extreme case that it took many years for my emotions to be healed, but now you would never know I was the same person. I love this new level of peace. I have seen and experienced thousands of astounding physical miracles. But to me, to have peace in my soul is the greatest miracle of all.

When your soul is healed, it will be like the one described in Psalm 131—as quiet as a weaned child.

SOUL WOUNDS CAUSE
TROUBLE IN RELATIONSHIPS

The wounds in your soul can cause trouble between you and your friends and family. Do you remember the story in the Bible of the incident at Ziklag? David was not yet ruler over Israel. In fact, he was on the run from King Saul. During that time he and a band of six hundred men and their wives and children were living in a town called Ziklag. Every day David and his men would go out and make raids against the enemies of Israel. One day they returned to Ziklag to find that the Amalekites had attacked them and taken everything, including the women and children (1 Sam. 30:1–5).

The Bible tells us that David's men blamed him for what happened and wanted to stone him: "David was greatly distressed, for the men spoke of stoning him because the souls of them all were bitterly grieved, each man for his sons and daughters" (1 Sam. 30:6, AMPC). David's men were ready to kill him! Was it his fault that the Amalekites took everyone? The Bible doesn't indicate that it was. Yet his men were ready to stone him for it. Why? First Samuel 30:6 says it was because their souls were "bitterly grieved."

It always amazes me what people do when their souls are wounded. They start throwing stones at others because of the pain they are feeling. David's men had followed him with all their hearts because he was a great leader and they believed in him. Yet as soon as they experienced a trauma, they became so wounded that they instantly turned on their beloved king and were going to kill him even though he was not to blame.

Imagine some of the things the men might have said that day. "This wouldn't have happened if David hadn't made us go out raiding. If we were home when the Amalekites came, we could have stopped it." Or "If David weren't in rebellion to Saul, we would be living safely in Israel far away from the Amalekites, and our wives and children would still be here."

Have you ever done anything similar to what David's men did? Something horrible happens, and immediately you start striking out at the people around you, even those you love. People fight because their souls are wounded by sins they have committed or traumas they have lived through. This is one of the biggest reasons we throw stones at one another.

It's also how divorce happens. Two wounded people get married and eventually turn against each other out of the unhealed areas in their souls. The fights that ensue make both of them even more wounded, and the resentment that forms in their hearts get so bad that they can no longer communicate in peace. Finally the marriage dissolves, and their children's lives are left in turmoil. If they only knew that their problems were coming from their souls, they could be healed, and their family would stay together.

Family members fight and marriages break apart because of junk in the soul realm. Churches split because of the wounded soul; businesses and ministries fail because of it. That's why we must learn how to be healed in our inner man.

SOUL WOUNDS CAUSE FINANCIAL FAILURE

Third John 2 says, "Beloved, I wish above all things that thou mayest prosper and be in health, even as thy soul prospereth" (KJV). Here, John is praying that you would prosper in all things. This doesn't refer only to spiritual prosperity but also to an increase in every area of your life, including your finances. The word "prosper" here is the Greek word *euodoō*, which means "to succeed in business affairs." [3]

It is God's will for you to be financially successful. But how? The secret lies in 3 John 2. This verse states that you will prosper *even as your soul prospers*. The health of your soul directly affects your ability to increase financially. Why? Your soul is made up of your mind, will, and emotions. If you have been wounded by sin or trauma, then your wounds will, in turn, control the way you think about money, the choices you make concerning your finances, and your spending habits.

Many believers are tithing faithfully as they petition God for supernatural alignment and blessings. However, they aren't seeing a breakthrough. The reason is because God can't trust them with the blessing while their soul is wounded. If He gave them the increase before they were healed, then the wounds inside their souls would sabotage everything they touched.

Let me give you a painful example. A wonderful couple I know came into a large inheritance and were unsure what to do with the money. They had a business they had been working on for a while but weren't certain they should launch it. They called and asked if I could help them discern the direction God wanted them to take. So I prayed, asking God to give them a word from Scripture or a dream that would get them on the right path.

A few days later the wife called me. She shared with me a dream she had in which she had been given a big beautiful diamond but zombies were trying to steal it from her. When she shared the dream, the Holy Spirit gave me the interpretation. The diamond represented their inheritance, and the zombies represented unhealed wounds in their souls that should have been long dead and buried but were "undead" and trying to eat their inheritance.

Immediately I advised them not to make any financial decisions until they could get some healing. They didn't listen. Instead, they launched their business, and it failed utterly. They ended up losing their entire inheritance. When I last talked to them, they couldn't even pay their mortgage.

A word to the wise: do not make any major purchases or investments or start a business or ministry until you first get some healing in your inner man. Once you do, you will prosper and be in health even as your soul is prospered.

SOUL WOUNDS CAUSE PHYSICAL SICKNESS

Third John 2 bears repeating: "Beloved, I wish above all things that thou mayest prosper and be in health, even as thy soul prospereth" (KJV). In this verse John also connects the health of your body to the prosperity of your soul.

Researchers are finding that people who experience childhood trauma are at a higher risk of developing life-threatening diseases as adults.[4] The Bible proves that diseases come from the wounded soul. In Psalm 41:4 the writer cries out, "LORD, be merciful unto me: heal my soul; for I have sinned against thee" (KJV). The same psalm assures us of God's healing by declaring, "The LORD will strengthen him upon the bed of languishing: thou wilt make all his bed in his sickness" (v. 3, KJV). So this psalm ties it all together. Sin wounds the soul and causes us to become physically sick, yet God promises to restore us from our bed of sickness!

Psalm 103 shows us the same truths.

> Bless the LORD, O my soul: and all that is within me, bless his holy name. Bless the LORD, O my soul, and forget not all his benefits: who forgiveth all thine iniquities; who healeth all thy diseases.
>
> —PSALM 103:1–3, KJV

Here the psalmist tells us that the Lord blesses our souls by forgiving us of all the iniquity and sin that has wounded us. Then He heals us of all the physical diseases that come from those wounds!

Soul wounds cause physical disease and disorder. Consider the story of the man at the pool of Bethesda. The Bible says there was a great multitude of sick people—blind, lame, and paralyzed—waiting at the pool for the moving of the water. An angel went down at a certain time into the pool and stirred up the water, and then whoever stepped in first was healed of whatever disease he had. A certain man who had an infirmity had been lying next to the pool for thirty-eight years (John 5:2–5).

When I first read this chapter, I wanted to know what made the man ill for that long. The answer lies in the language used in the story. The word "infirmity"—*astheneia* in Greek—means "want of strength, weakness, infirmity...of the soul."[5]

He had a wound in his soul that caused his physical body to be sick for almost four decades. How did he get wounded? Later on, after the man is healed, Jesus ran into him in the temple and said, "See, you have been made well. Sin no more, lest a worse thing come upon you" (v. 14). By Jesus's words we can discern that sin wounded this man's soul then caused him to be infirm in his body.

Does the Bible tell us what his sin was? I think we can discern that answer through the conversation Jesus had with the man when He healed him. Let's look at it.

> When Jesus saw him lying there, and knew that he already had been in that condition a long time, He said to him, "Do you want to be made well?" The sick man answered Him, "Sir, I have no man to put me into the pool when the water is stirred up; but while I am coming, another steps down before me."
>
> —JOHN 5:6–7

If I had been sick for thirty-eight years and someone asked me if I wanted to be well, I would have screamed, "Yes!" with all my might, but not this guy. He told Jesus he had no one to put him in the pool, and when the water was stirred, everybody else there cut in line in front of him.

One day when I was reading this story, the Lord showed me how offended that man had gotten after being sick for so long and having none of his family and friends around to help him. His conversation with Jesus could have very well gone like this:

"I have no one to put me into the pool when the water is stirred. None of my family or friends ever stay here with me to wait for the angel to come. They drop me off in the morning with this ratty mat and not even a bologna sandwich.

"And that's not all. Even though every other sick person at the pool knows I have been here the longest, they still cut in front of me when the water is stirred. You'd think they would give me first dibs because I've been here so long, but no…"

I believe this man's sin was that he had become very offended. Offense is one of the primary sins I see wounding people and making them sick.

I remember a young man who received a miracle in one of my meetings. He had a horrible sinus infection that hadn't let up for over a year. He said it was so bad it stunk, and even other people could smell it. The day he came to my meeting, I was teaching about how offense wounds the soul and makes you sick. He later told me that as soon as he prayed the soul-healing prayers, the infection dried up and the smell totally disappeared.

One woman who came to one of my meetings knew she was offended but never connected the offense with the trouble she was having with her gums. Every time she brushed, her gums would bleed profusely. Yet when she prayed the soul-healing prayers, a creative miracle happened. That night as she brushed there was no bleeding. Startled, she looked at her gums and was shocked to find they were a beautiful, healthy pink and had grown back completely.

Soul Wounds Cause Demonic Assaults

Wounds in your soul can not only make you physically sick; they can also give demonic spirits the right to attack every part of your life, including your physical body. Look at this story about the woman bowed over in Luke:

> And, behold, there was a woman which had a spirit of infirmity eighteen years, and was bowed together, and could in no wise lift up herself. And when Jesus saw her, he called her to him, and said unto her, Woman, thou art loosed from thine infirmity. And he laid his hands on her: and immediately she was made straight, and glorified God.
>
> —Luke 13:11–13, kjv

This woman had an evil spirit that was attacking her physical body. What gave that demon the right to literally bend her spine? The Bible tells us it was a spirit of infirmity. The word "infirmity" here is the same word used to describe the man at the pool (*astheneia* in Greek). It means "weakness, infirmity of the body...of the soul."[6] She had a wound in her soul that was giving the demon a legal right to torment her.

A woman who attended one of my meetings has a similar story. She came up to testify of a deliverance and miracle she had experienced while receiving soul healing in the meeting. She had fractured her back in a boating accident twenty years before. Since that time she would experience a gripping and pinching on one side of her back if she stood longer than five minutes. She said she had been prayed for more than one hundred times with no breakthrough or relief whatsoever.

During the meeting I had everyone lie down and focus on Jesus healing their souls. While on the floor she was shifting around a lot because of the pain, but then suddenly her leg jerked, and the pain she had suffered from for so long was completely gone. When she came to testify, she said that when the jerk happened, it felt as if "something" left. She believed that as she was getting her soul healed, a spirit that had been afflicting her finally departed.

That woman experienced the same thing the woman bent over went through. She had a spirit of infirmity on her that left when Jesus healed her soul and then loosed her of its power! When sin or trauma wounds you, it gives demonic powers the right to attack you. Ephesians 6:12 (KJV) backs up this statement:

> For we wrestle not against flesh and blood, but against principalities, against powers, against the rulers of the darkness of this world, against spiritual wickedness in high places.

According to this verse, the spirits we wrestle with rule over the darkness of this world. Is that "darkness" referring only to the evil that exists beyond ourselves? That's part of it, but according to the meaning of the word *darkness*, demonic spirits also get the right to rule in our personal lives because of the unhealed areas in our souls.

The word "darkness" is the Greek word *skotos*. It means "the soul has lost its perceptive powers."[7] What would make your soul lose its ability to perceive things correctly? It is wounds that came from sins, trauma, and generational issues. Those unhealed areas bring darkness to your mind, will, and emotions. They cause you to think wrong thoughts, make wrong decisions, and feel bad, negative emotions so that you perceive things incorrectly. The darkness in your wounded soul is what gives evil powers the right to rule over your life.

Even the strongman—Satan—will be defeated when your

soul gets healed. The strongman holds the most powerful position in the demonic kingdom. He is over a house of demons that have been assigned to harass, torment, and even kill you. The Bible says the only way to defeat him and ransack his house is by binding him. "Or else how can one enter into a strong man's house, and spoil his goods, except he first bind the strong man? And then he will spoil his house" (Matt. 12:29, KJV).

How do you do that? The answer is contained in the meaning of the word *strongman*. It's the Greek word *ischyros*, which, when referring to Satan, means "strong, mighty." [8] But it can also mean "one who has strength of soul to sustain the attacks of Satan, strong and therefore exhibiting many excellences." [9] So in order to bind and defeat the Strongman, you must have "strength of soul." As you are healed in your inner man, you will be able not only to resist his attack but also to exercise spiritual authority over him to bind him and thoroughly ransack all the spirits in his house.

SOUL WOUNDS CAUSE LONG-TERM DISORDERS AND PREVENT HEALING

Both the man at the pool and the woman bent over were sick for a very long time because of the unhealed areas in their souls. Their examples demonstrate that not only can soul wounds make you sick, but also they can keep you sick for years until you recognize your need for healing and seek it. I have interviewed countless people who suffered for twenty, thirty, and even fifty years with an affliction of some kind, and no matter what they tried, they were not cured. Yet when they were healed in their inner man, their physical healing manifested immediately.

When I ministered in Horseheads, New York, people were

healed of a large variety of issues. The group included a man who was a retired lieutenant who had worked in seventy prisons throughout the state. He had injured his shoulder in a scuffle in prison and had been in pain for thirty years. When I heard him tell his story, I felt as if the traumatic incident had also wounded his soul. Once he received healing in his inner man during the activation, he got a breakthrough. He came up on stage and demonstrated his miracle by rotating his arm around and around with full movement and not a bit of pain.

In another place I was calling out words of knowledge while commanding people's souls to be healed. My declarations started a movement of people running around the room to demonstrate their healings. One of them was a man who had severe breathing problems for more than fifty years. In the meeting he realized that the Lord had healed his soul, so he took a step of faith by running around the conference hall until he was totally healed. Later while onstage he described the wonderful freedom he felt as he easily took in breaths after not being able to do so for more than five decades.

One woman had sustained a sports-related injury more than twenty years before. Throughout those long and painful years she felt constant strain and stress in her neck and had to visit a chiropractor regularly. What the doctor did helped relieve some of the effects of the injury, but it was Jesus who took her pain away for good. During the meeting she felt a moist cooling rolling off her shoulders as she was healed of the trauma from her accident, and the tension and pain she had lived with constantly for twenty years was gone.

As these stories demonstrate, wounds in the soul that come from traumas, sins, and generational issues can prevent a person from being healed of a disease or injury—often for a very long time. That is why a lot of people with sports injuries or those who have been in car wrecks never fully recover physically. They don't realize that the trauma they went through wounded them in their souls and the wound they received is preventing them from getting well.

It's possible that there are unhealed areas in your soul that are keeping you from receiving a miracle. So let's look at how you can be healed through the power of Jesus Christ.

PRAYER ACTIVATION

As we move forward, let's pray together so soul healing can begin to manifest in your life. Say this decree out loud:

> *Lord Jesus, I believe that even now You are healing me of every wound in my soul that is driving me to sin, that is determining who I am and controlling what I say. I believe every wound that is causing my emotions to be unbalanced is being healed. I decree that You are healing every wound in me that is ruining my relationships, sabotaging my finances, making me physically sick, and even opening me up to demonic attack. I also believe that any long-term illnesses I have been suffering from are going to finally be healed as You prosper me in health even as my soul is prospered. I thank You, Lord, for the amazing victory You are bringing me now. In Jesus's name I pray, amen.*

Chapter 4

THE FINISHED WORK OF CHRIST: THE CROSS

Y OU'VE PROBABLY FIGURED out by this point in the book that soul wounds have the ability to totally devastate our lives. But the Bible has good news for us: God promises to heal our wounded souls. Psalm 147:3 says, "He heals the broken-hearted and binds up their wounds."

Hebrew translation of this verse uses the phrase "broken in heart" rather than our one English word *brokenhearted*. The words "in heart" (Hebrew *leb*) mean the soul.[1] So in essence you could rewrite this scripture to read, "He heals the broken in *soul* by binding up their wounds."

This is an encouraging word considering the devastation soul wounds can bring. The question is, how does God bind up our wounds, and are there ways we can partner with Him to get a breakthrough?

Thankfully the Lord has given us powerful soul-healing weapons that we have free access to. The Bible alludes to them in 2 Corinthians:

> (For the weapons of our warfare are not carnal, but mighty through God to the pulling down of strong holds;) Casting down imaginations, and every high thing that exalteth itself against the knowledge of God,

and bringing into captivity every thought to the obedi-
ence of Christ.

—2 CORINTHIANS 10:4–5, KJV

Christians around the world quote this verse all the time
without realizing that it is talking about soul healing. It says
God has given us "mighty" weapons to pull down strongholds
in our minds and bring every thought into captivity to Christ.
The word "mighty" is the Greek word *dynatos*, which means
"strong in soul."[2] So the weapons that bring down strongholds
in your inner being are ones that make your soul strong, and
they all come out of the finished work of Jesus Christ.

We will discuss one of these powerful weapons in this
chapter and more in the chapters to come.

THE CROSS

I have walked through nearly a decade of soul healing, and
during that time I have learned a very important lesson: *the
key to total healing is to believe on the finished work of Christ.*
One aspect of that finished work is the Cross. The Bible tells
us that in Jesus's final moments on the cross He said, "It is
finished!" before bowing His head and giving up His spirit
(John 19:30).

When Jesus said, "It is finished," He wasn't referring only
to the pain and suffering He endured during the crucifixion.
He was saying that in that very moment our redemption and
everything that came with it was complete. He took all our
sin upon Himself and paid off the debt we owed to the Father.
In other words, though we deserved death as the punishment
for our sins, Jesus took our place and died for us. This is great
news! As Charles Spurgeon once explained, your sins cannot

be in two places at once. They are either on you, or they are on Christ![3]

Many scriptures state that Jesus died "once for all" for sin. Here are two:

> For the death that He died, He died to sin once for all; but the life that He lives, He lives to God.
>
> —ROMANS 6:10

> For indeed Christ died for sins once for all, the Just and Righteous for the unjust and unrighteous [the Innocent for the guilty] so that He might bring us to God, having been put to death in the flesh, but made alive in the Spirit.
>
> —1 PETER 3:18, AMP

Jesus had to die only once for all your sins—past, present, and future. This means you are already forgiven, even for the sins you are yet to commit. His work is done. He doesn't have to come down from heaven and crawl back up on the cross every time you blow it.

At Calvary, Jesus also filled the prophecy in Isaiah 53:4–5:

> Surely He has borne our griefs and carried our sorrows; yet we esteemed Him stricken, smitten by God, and afflicted. But He was wounded for our transgressions, He was bruised for our iniquities; the chastisement for our peace was upon Him, and by His stripes we are healed.

In one fell swoop Jesus did it all. He gave His life for every sin, sickness, curse, pain, separation, and devastation you will ever face. Yet most Christians are not living in the finished work of Christ. We continue to try to do things to make ourselves pleasing and acceptable to God even though Jesus drank the cup of God's righteous wrath all the way down to the dregs. We also continue to live with all sorts of maladies even though Jesus paid a great price to deliver us from them.

Not many believers have been able to truly grasp the finished work. Are you fighting cancer? Jesus healed you two thousand years ago when He took the stripes on His back. Is your family under a financial curse? It has already been broken because Jesus became a curse for you so you could have the blessings of Abraham. Yet when we pray, we beg God to heal and prosper us. I'll let you in on a secret: there is no need to beg God to do something He has already done.

The Bible says, "According as his divine power [God] hath given unto us all things that pertain unto life and godliness, through the knowledge of him that hath called us to glory and virtue" (2 Peter 1:3, KJV). This verse makes it clear that we have *already* been given all things that pertain to life. When the Bible says "all," it doesn't mean *some*; it means *everything*. Notice these blessings were *given* to us. The word *given* denotes a gift. Last time I checked, you don't have to work for gifts; you receive them for free, no strings attached. Yet we continue to try to earn God's help and His blessing through excessive religious rituals.

FAITH VS. WORKS

There is nothing wrong with spiritual disciplines such as fasting and prayer. Indeed, both are vital in our walk with the Lord.

Prayer is our means of intimate communication with Him. However, we should never keep track of every hour we spend in prayer as though we can chalk up favor with God by engaging in it.

Fasting is the same. Jesus said "this kind" (meaning a

certain sort of demon) comes out only through prayer and fasting (Mark 9:29). He was telling us that fasting helps us battle and win against demonic spirits. But it does not move God to remove a spirit from you. Jesus already did that when He made a public spectacle of the enemy at the cross. Now it's up to you to pick up the authority He won for you and use it to break the enemy's hold off your life.

We wrongly think of fasting as a way to win God's love and approval. Yet fasting is not a practice that moves *God*; rather, it helps *us*! David said he afflicted, or humbled, his soul with fasting (Ps. 35:13), meaning it was a tool he used to get the unholy behaviors in his soul to die. Fasting helps us act right, but it is Jesus who made us righteous by taking on all our sin.

Walking the line between Spirit-led works and works of the flesh is like being on a balance beam. Go too far one way, and you could fall off and hurt yourself. The Bible says that when we enter into our own works, we can be cursed (Gal. 3:10)!

During my adventures in soul healing I have fallen off the beam many times. There was a long season during which I kept thinking that if I fasted and prayed excessively, God would be pleased and grant me the breakthrough I sought. However, during those times I didn't experience the supernatural power of God. Instead, things started going downhill fast. I got sick, busted, and disgusted. That's when God led me to this stunning verse:

> And all who depend on the Law [who are seeking to be justified by obedience to the Law of rituals] are under a curse and doomed to disappointment and destruction.
> —Galatians 3:10, ampc

I was doing exactly what this scripture warns against— seeking to be pleasing to God by earning my breakthrough

through religious rituals. Yet the Bible says we are justified by our faith in Christ and His finished work! Without faith it's impossible to please God. The result of my religious rituals was that I was cursed instead of blessed. No wonder things were getting bad!

Many of us have fallen into the trap of using our own strength and works to try to make God love us more and thus do something amazing for us. But Jesus already did it all when He gave His life. If things are getting worse rather than better for you, there is a possibility that you have cursed yourself through excessive religious rituals. The apostle Paul wrote a stunning rebuke to the Galatians, who had fallen into this trap:

> O foolish Galatians! Who has bewitched you that you should not obey the truth, before whose eyes Jesus Christ was clearly portrayed among you as crucified? This only I want to learn from you: Did you receive the Spirit by the works of the law, or by the hearing of faith? Are you so foolish? Having begun in the Spirit, are you now being made perfect by the flesh? Have you suffered so many things in vain—if indeed it was in vain? Therefore He who supplies the Spirit to you and works miracles among you, does He do it by the works of the law, or by the hearing of faith?
>
> —GALATIANS 3:1–5

Our salvation began by grace through faith, not by works. So why have we switched over to thinking that now we must rely on our own efforts to live rightly? The Bible says our own righteousness is as filthy rags (Isa. 64:6). Do you want miracles in your life? Galatians 3:5 tells you how to get them. God works miracles among us not through the works of the law but by our faith in Christ's finished work on the cross!

We must cease from our works and unsanctified rituals birthed in wrong motives and instead *labor* to enter into His rest through believing. This revelation was the catalyst for major soul healing in my life.

BELIEVE AND ENTER INTO HIS REST

When you believe and receive all Jesus has already done for you, then you enter into the rest of God and cross over into your promised land. Canaan was the inheritance God gave to His people that was full of cool stuff they didn't have to work for—wells they didn't dig, houses they didn't build, and vineyards they didn't plant.

God has a promised resting place for you too. It is an inheritance full of soul healing, divine health, prosperity, joy, and abundant life that you don't earn but rather receive for free by grace because of Christ's sacrifice. Hebrews 4 says:

> Therefore, while the promise of entering His rest still remains and is freely offered today, let us fear, in case any one of you may seem to come short of reaching it or think he has come too late. For indeed we have had the good news [of salvation] preached to us, just as the Israelites also [when the good news of the promised land came to them]; but the message they heard did not benefit them, because it was not united with faith [in God] by those who heard. For we who believe [that is, we who personally trust and confidently rely on God] enter that rest [so we have His inner peace now because we are confident in our salvation, and assured of His power].
>
> —HEBREWS 4:1–3, AMP

When the good news of the Promised Land was preached to the Israelites, they did not unite it with their faith in God. They refused to enter in because of fear and unbelief, and they ended up wandering in the desert for forty more years because of it.

You don't want to make the same mistake. The good news of salvation has been preached to us, so don't allow unbelief to cause you to come short of entering the rest of Christ. The key to entering in is to have faith in His finished work and receive all it has accomplished. There is nothing wrong with fasting and praying, but when you use it to try to get God to move you into your promised land, you will end up wandering in your desert too.

SOUL-HEALING REST

When you begin to truly understand what Jesus accomplished through His sacrifice, it will bring peace and rest to your soul. Look again at this portion of Hebrews 4:

> For we who believe [that is, we who personally trust and confidently rely on God] enter that rest [so we have His inner peace now because we are confident in our salvation, and assured of His power].
>
> —HEBREWS 4:3, AMP

When you walk in the finished work of Christ through your faith, then you enter into His rest. This will cause you to have His inner peace in your soul! To me there is nothing more important than this. If you took everything away from me and said I could have only one thing back, I would ask for soul peace because then I would have it all! I would prosper and be in health even as my soul prospers.

When you labor to live in the finished work of Christ, you will find rest for your wounded soul. Look at what Jesus said about this:

> Take My yoke upon you and learn from Me, for I am gentle and lowly in heart, and you will find rest for your souls.
>
> —MATTHEW 11:28–29

What yoke is Jesus referring to? Believing in Him and all He has done! This yoking with Christ's finished work brings an indescribable amount of rest into your life. The word "rest" here is the Greek word *anapausis*, which literally means "blessed tranquility of soul."[4] This verse proves that soul healing comes from believing!

Believing in the finished work of Christ causes soul prosperity to come easy because it means every wound you encounter has already been healed. As you genuinely believe this statement is true because of Christ's finished work, then your healing will manifest.

Many times God will show me an unhealed place in my soul through a dream or while I am studying the Scriptures. I also receive insights by just tuning in to how I am feeling inside myself. If my mind isn't quiet and my emotions are in turmoil, I know something is going on in my inner man. I might not know exactly what it is, but that's when I use my faith to believe that Jesus has already paid the price to heal it. As I start decreeing scriptures about the finished work of Christ over my soul, I suddenly feel a sense of peace and assurance come over me. That's when I know that I just received a supernatural healing in my inner man.

The best way to grow your faith to enter into His rest is through studying, meditating on, and decreeing the finished works of Jesus. The Bible says that "faith comes by hearing, and hearing by the word of God" (Rom. 10:17). The more you read the scriptures about what Jesus *has already done*, the more your faith will rise to believe it. Then as you decree His work over your situations, you will see major breakthroughs. The result is that you will become confident in your salvation and the power that is available to you in God, including all Christ has done to heal your soul.

Here are just a few things Jesus completed at the cross. Meditate on them, and decree them over your life and your soul.

- By His stripes I am already healed (Isa. 53:5).

- He was risen to life so I could have new life (Rom. 4:25).

- He put my old man to death (Rom. 6:6).

- He is the lover of my soul (Rom. 8:31–39).

- In Him all the promises of God are yes and amen (2 Cor. 1:20).

- In Him I am a new creation (2 Cor. 5:17).

- He reconciled me to God (2 Cor. 5:18).

- Jesus endured my poverty that I might share His abundance (2 Cor. 8:9).

- He became a curse so I could have the blessings of Abraham (Gal. 3:13–14).

- He went down in death so I could die (to sin) with Him (1 Pet. 2:24).

- He took on my sin so I could be made His righteousness (1 Pet. 2:24).

- He gave up His life so that I might be forgiven (1 John 3:16).

How Do We "Cease From Our Own Works"?

I think the reason Christians find it difficult to enter God's rest and therefore fall off the balance beam between religious rituals and Spirit-birthed works is that they don't know how to discern the difference between the two. Let's go to Hebrews 4 again to find some help.

> For he that is entered into his rest, he also hath ceased from his own works, as God did from his. Let us labour therefore to enter into that rest, lest any man fall after the same example of unbelief.
>
> —Hebrews 4:10–11, kjv

This scripture seems to contradict itself. On one hand it says we must cease from our own works, but on the other it directs us to "labour" to enter into God's rest. How can we cease from works and labor at the same time?

Ceasing from your works means not using fasting, prayer, and other rituals to try to get God to be pleased with you or to make Him do something you want Him to do—for example, heal you or prosper you. There is nothing you can do to make God love you more or bless you more. After all, while you were still a sinner Christ died for you (Rom. 5:8) and made available to you everything necessary for "life and godliness" (2 Pet. 1:3).

Ceasing from your own works also means to stop making

statements that sound as though Jesus's work is not finished. You are expressing unbelief when you make comments such as, "Oh, God, please heal my body!" Instead use your mouth to labor to enter into His rest by decreeing the truth of the Word over your situation: "Lord, by Your stripes I am already healed" (Isa. 53:5; 1 Pet. 2:24).

These faith decrees are how you labor to enter into His rest. It takes great effort to say you are already healed when you were just diagnosed with cancer. Trust me, I know. It seems insane to say you're not sick when your doctors say you're going to die! But this is the way you labor to enter into His rest. You keep decreeing the truth about Christ's finished work over your situation, and when you feel fear, anxiety, and doubt break off, you know you have entered His rest. Don't forget: that place of rest is your promised land, where the manifestation of your hopes and dreams is.

PRAYER ACTIVATION

Below are prayers I fashioned for you based on Christ's completed work. Pray these often, and don't forget to decree them over your life and soul.

> Lord, I cease from my own works of excessive religious rituals, fear, and unbelief, and I choose instead to labor to enter into Your rest through my faith in Christ's finished work and biblical decrees.

> I believe and decree the truth that Jesus has already shed His blood once for all for all my sin and that His sacrifice on the cross is a finished work. Through Christ I have already been given everything I need for life and godliness [Rom. 6:10; 1 Pet. 3:18].

Lord, I yoke myself to Your finished work. As I learn about what You have already done for me, I will find blessed tranquility and rest for my soul [Matt. 11:29].

I believe God demonstrated His own love for me in this: while I was still a sinner, Christ died for me [Rom. 5:8].

Jesus, when You died on the cross, You said, "It is finished." You died to sin once for all, the just for the unjust, so that You might bring me to God. I have been put to death in the flesh but made alive in the spirit. I gratefully rest in Your completed work [John 19:30; 1 Pet. 3:18].

Jesus, You knew no sin, yet You became sin on my behalf so that I might become the righteousness of God in You [2 Cor. 5:21].

Jesus, You canceled out my sin and the certificate of debt, consisting of decrees that were against me, by taking it out of the way, having nailed it to the cross [Col. 2:14].

Jesus, You bore my sins in Your body on the cross, that I might die to sin and live to righteousness; for by Your stripes I am already healed [1 Pet. 2:24].

Chapter 5

THE FINISHED WORK OF CHRIST: THE BLOOD OF JESUS

THE SECOND MIGHTY weapon of God related to the finished work of Christ that makes your soul strong is the blood of Jesus. The Bible says that Jesus shed His blood at the cross for every sin, which includes those that wounded your soul. In fact, He shed His blood not only to defeat sin, the curse, and death and to give us eternal life but also to give us the power to heal our inner man.

Matthew 8:17 says Jesus died "that it might be fulfilled which was spoken by Isaiah the prophet, saying: 'He Himself took our infirmities and bore our sicknesses.'" His death is the fulfillment of the promise given in Isaiah 53 that says through His sacrifice Jesus took our infirmities. Again, that word *infirmity* means "weakness, infirmity of the soul."[1] This verse in Matthew proves that Jesus died to heal the wounds in your inner man!

When the Lord shed His blood on the cross, He washed away every sin that put a wound in your soul. Leviticus 17:11 (KJV) says:

> For the life of the flesh is in the blood: and I have given it to you upon the altar to make an atonement for your souls: for it is the blood that maketh an atonement for the soul.

This verse twice makes the point that the blood atones for the soul. That's because the soul is where sin lives. When believers hear the phrase *being led by the flesh*, they mistakenly think their physical bodies are causing them to sin. But that is incorrect. Your body does whatever your mind thinks about, your will chooses, and your emotions lead you to do. The flesh refers to the carnal nature, which resides in your soul. Leviticus says the blood atones for the soul because it's your inner man that needs to be washed clean by the blood so you can walk in the uprightness Jesus already won for you.

The blood is an important step in soul healing because it totally removes the sin that created your wounds, and it also cleanses every part of your inner man.

Hebrews 9:14 makes this truth clear.

> How much more shall the blood of Christ, who through the eternal Spirit offered Himself without spot to God, cleanse your conscience from dead works to serve the living God?

The word "conscience" is the Greek word *syneidēsis*, which means "the soul."[2] The blood is the most powerful soap in the universe! It literally cleanses your inner man of every sin and anything that is bringing defilement upon your mind, will, and emotions. So if your mind is full of noise, you are making bad decisions, or your emotions are a mess, then decree that your soul is being washed with the blood, and watch as God cleanses and removes those painful afflictions and brings peace to every part of your inner being.

THE BLOOD CLEANSES YOUR BLOODLINE

The sins your ancestors committed centuries ago could be causing you massive problems today. As we discussed earlier, their wounds were passed down to you while you were being formed in the womb. Because Satan can strategically use those wounds to cause poverty, sickness, and even death in your life, you must be healed of your ancestral issues. The first step to healing is applying the blood of Jesus.

Romans 3:25 proves that Jesus became a propitiation for every sin your ancestors committed in the past.

> God hath set forth [His Son] to be a propitiation through faith in his blood, to declare his righteousness for the remission of sins that are past, through the forbearance of God.
>
> —ROMANS 3:25, KJV

The blood of Jesus is so powerful that it travels back in time through your bloodline to totally wipe out every past sin all the way to Adam. Some of the biggest physical and financial battles Christians face today stem from their pasts. Even doctors in the natural will ask for the history of disease in your family because they know that many of the sicknesses you are dealing with were passed down from your ancestors.

A huge percentage of the battles I have waged and diseases I have been hit with came from wounds I received in the womb. When Holy Spirit showed me those things, I would start the soul-healing process by declaring Romans 3:25 over them. That is how I would labor to enter into His rest.

Every time the Lord shows you something in your soul that was passed down to you from your family, start your healing with the decrees at the end of this chapter. Then follow up with the powerful tool I will show you in the next chapter.

THE BLOOD AND THE CROSS
STOP THE DEVIL

When Jesus shed His blood on the cross, He defeated death and the one who had its power, Satan.

> Therefore, since the children share in flesh and blood, He Himself likewise also partook of the same, that through death He might render powerless him who had the power of death, that is, the devil.
> —HEBREWS 2:14, NASB

The devil once held the power to kill us. In fact, today he still tries to fulfill his mandate to steal, kill, and destroy (John 10:10), but ultimately he has been stripped of his right to do so because of the shed blood of Jesus! If this is true, why do we still see demonically based sickness and disease taking people out? Because there are unhealed areas in their souls that give Satan the legal right to attack them and because they do not fully believe that Christ's work on the cross and His shed blood defeated him.

One aspect of laboring to enter into His rest is meditating on verses such as Hebrews 2:14 until they become truth to you. I highly encourage you to decree this verse in particular over your life every day to remind yourself and Satan that he does not hold the power of death anymore so he has no ability to take your life. This laboring through Christ's death and His shed blood will also bring healing to the places in your soul the enemy is using as a legal right to kill you!

THE BLOOD AND THE CROSS
DESTROY CONDEMNATION

For some reason Christians embrace feeling condemned even though the Bible says there is no condemnation in Christ (Rom. 8:1). We are under the mistaken impression that if we don't let ourselves feel this way, then we aren't truly sorry for our sins. But ask yourself: Does being condemned make you holy? The answer is a resounding no. It is faith in Christ's finished work on the cross and His blood that justify you.

Do you realize that when you let yourself walk in condemnation, you are sinning? You are not believing the truth about the power of the blood and what Christ accomplished, and the Bible says "whatever is not from faith is sin" (Rom. 14:23). God will never make you feel condemned—ever! There is a big difference between condemnation and conviction. When God brings conviction, you will know it because you will have godly sorrow for your sin, which will lead you to faith-filled repentance. As you step into His correction, you will feel the freedom and refreshing that comes from receiving His loving discipline.

Revelation 12:10 calls Satan "the accuser of our brethren" because condemnation is one of his favorite tools. Every day the devil will put thoughts in your mind of how wicked and sinful your soul is. Night and day he will ruthlessly criticize and find fault with the things you say and the way you act. You must learn to recognize his voice and firmly and aggressively reject it; you have the legal right to do so as a blood-bought child of God.

You will know the devil is on an assignment to accuse you when you feel weighed down with guilt and shame. His mental assaults can be so fierce they make you feel overwhelmed. That's when you use the scriptures to combat his attack. When you labor to enter into God's rest, you are resisting Satan, so he will have to flee.

When the devil tries to make me feel condemned, I use the truth of the cross and the blood as weapons against him. I get in his face with the facts. Colossians 2:13–15 tells us what those are.

> And you, being dead in your trespasses and the uncircumcision of your flesh, He has made alive together with Him, having forgiven you all trespasses, having wiped out the handwriting of requirements that was against us, which was contrary to us. And He has taken it out of the way, having nailed it to the cross. Having disarmed principalities and powers, He made a public spectacle of them, triumphing over them in it.

When the devil comes at you, he always brings a list of your sins, both old and new. His only weapon is sin that has not been forgiven. However, Christ took this power away from him when He poured out His blood for every sin you have ever committed. This includes the list of "handwritten requirements" that were against you. Because of the forgiveness Jesus won for you, that list is null and void, and the enemy has been disarmed and made a public spectacle of!

Learn to recognize condemnation because the devil doesn't play fair. He will try to make you think that you are not forgiven of the sins that wounded you. If you hear his condemning voice while you are seeking your breakthrough, reject it. Then labor to enter into God's rest by decreeing all the scriptures that say your sins are already under the blood.

In what other ways can we appropriate the power of the cross and the blood to our souls? It's important to combine your faith in Christ's finished work with the act of repentance.

REPENTANCE

The Greek word for repent is *metanoeō*, which means "to change one's mind for better, heartily to amend with abhorrence of one's past sins."[3] When we repent to God, we are not simply saying "I'm sorry" but are acknowledging that we loathe our sins and are promising to turn from the ways we were thinking and acting. God's Word promises that if we do this, God forgives us. "If we confess our sins, he is faithful and just to forgive us our sins, and to cleanse us from all unrighteousness" (1 John 1:9, KJV).

I love having the right to repent. If you have ever lost it on someone, then you know that afterward you feel as if you took a roll in the mud. Yet 1 John 1:9 assures us that repentance cleanses us of our unrighteous behavior and the icky feeling that comes with it. Repentance is not just for God; it is for us too. After you repent, you always feel refreshed and clean.

However, the Bible also tells us that if we are drawn away by our flesh and do not repent, we give birth to sin, which results in death.

> Let no one say when he is tempted, "I am tempted by God"; for God cannot be tempted by evil, nor does He Himself tempt anyone. But each one is tempted when he is drawn away by his own desires and enticed. Then, when desire has conceived, it gives birth to sin; and sin, when it is full-grown, brings forth death."
>
> —JAMES 1:13–15

The word "death" in this passage is the Greek word *thanatos*, which means "the misery of the soul arising from sin."[4] Sin has consequences. It wounds you, brings pain and misery to your soul, and opens the door for demonic oppression.

When you repent, you are partaking of the power of the cross and applying the blood of Jesus, which will slam that door shut and heal your soul.

Many teachers say we don't need to repent anymore because of the finished work of Christ. However, 1 John 1:9 makes it clear that we are forgiven of our sins *if we confess them.* Acts 3 confirms this truth:

> Repent ye therefore, and be converted, that your sins may be blotted out, when the times of refreshing shall come from the presence of the Lord.
>
> —ACTS 3:19, KJV

Repentance brings refreshment! Think about it! It feels great to be unburdened of your sin. Repentance takes the load off! It causes you to change your mind and behavior and brings you into a wide place of rest and freedom.

In Psalm 51 we see a wonderful example of repentance bringing refreshment. Here David is repenting for his sins of murder and adultery.

> Have mercy upon me, O God, according to Your lovingkindness; according to the multitude of Your tender mercies, blot out my transgressions. Wash me thoroughly from my iniquity, and cleanse me from my sin. For I acknowledge my transgressions, and my sin is always before me.
>
> —PSALM 51:1–3

David was laboring to enter into the rest of God through his repentance. After confessing he said, "Restore to me the joy of Your salvation" (v. 12). He understood that the gift of repentance returns to us the joy we first experienced upon our regeneration.

Refreshment and joy are the fruit of true, God-granted repentance. If you don't have that kind of manifestation, then you have turned repentance into a work. If you are excessively pleading the blood of Jesus and continuing to feel condemned and guilty afterward, then you are doing your own work instead of laboring to enter into His rest.

When I first started to get my soul healed, I would spend endless hours repenting of the sins that had wounded my soul. During those times I always felt as if it was never enough. The weight of my sin was so heavy that I was always left feeling condemned no matter how much I confessed.

One day in the middle of this process I saw a vision. I was trapped in a laundry machine that was stuck on the wash cycle. I saw myself churning around and around and literally drowning in the sudsy water. I came out of the vision panting in panic and immediately heard the Lord say, "Enough repenting; now believe!"

We can turn repenting into a work by not believing in Christ's finished work while we do it. Even Judas repented but then afterward hung himself because his repentance was not combined with faith in Christ. Rather it was based on the awareness of his guilt, the devil's condemnation, and the requirements of the law.

You must learn to strike a balance when pursuing soul healing. The blood is what wipes out the sin in your soul that wounded you. So starting with repentance and the blood immediately brings healing power into your inner man. Yet don't turn your repentance into a work. Make sure you keep in your heart the truth that you are already forgiven. Then use your repentance to labor to enter into God's rest. Make biblical decrees about how the blood has already washed away your sin rather than begging God to forgive you. He has already done that.

FORGIVENESS HEALS THE SOUL

In addition to repenting of your own sins, you must also forgive those who have sinned against you. Unforgiveness wounds your soul and causes problems of every kind. And it's not optional. The Bible says we are to forgive others as Christ forgave us, "forbearing one another, and forgiving one another, if any man have a quarrel against any: even as Christ forgave you, so also do ye" (Col. 3:13, KJV).

One of the surest ways to wound yourself is by holding on to unforgiveness! If you're doing that, you need to let it go. It doesn't matter what others have done to you. When you refuse to forgive them, you hurt yourself! I have seen people experience amazing physical miracles when they let go of an offense and forgave someone.

A woman who came to one of my meetings was very offended at a close friend of hers, though she tried to maintain the friendship. A week or so before the event, she lost a filling, which left a hole in her tooth. She said it was so deep she could put her tongue into it. That morning I was teaching on offense and suddenly got a word of knowledge that enamel was growing into people's teeth. As soon as I said the word about the enamel, she felt pain in her tooth. When she tried to push her tongue into it, she discovered the hole was no longer there. She went to the bathroom and checked several times before she finally came up to testify. The miracle happened right after her soul was healed of offense.

Whenever I catch myself holding on to someone's wrongs, I try to quickly repent and forgive that person so I can keep my soul in good health. It's important for you to do the same.

The cross and the blood of Christ are the beginning of soul healing, but there is another key you must have in order to experience total freedom. We'll learn about it in the next chapter.

PRAYER ACTIVATION

Use these decrees to begin your healing. Declare that the blood of Jesus Christ has already washed away your sin.

> I decree that Jesus took on all the infirmities in my soul and body when He went to the cross. That means every wound in me is already healed because of His finished work. Now because I believe, my healing is going to manifest [Matt. 8:17].

> I decree that when the Lord shed His blood on the cross, He washed away every sin that put a wound in my inner man. Leviticus 17:11 says the blood atones for my soul, so right now His blood is washing me clean of every sin that has wounded me.

> As I confess my sin, He is faithful and just to forgive me and cleanse me from all unrighteousness [1 John 1:9].

> I decree that right now the blood of Christ is cleansing my conscience and every area of my soul from dead works to serve the living God. I also decree that the blood is wiping out every sin from the past that came to me through my family bloodline. As I repent of all sin, times of refreshing will come [Heb. 9:14; Rom. 3:25; Acts 3:19].

By the power of the blood, I also forgive anyone who has ever hurt me. I forgive just as Christ forgave me [Col. 3:13].

I decree that through the cross and the blood, Jesus took away the power of the one who had the power of death; that is, the devil. So Satan has no legal right to take my life through tragedy or disease [Heb. 2:14].

I resist any condemning thought Satan is putting in my mind. I decree that the handwriting of requirements that was against me, the list Satan is using to accuse me, is under the blood. It was nailed to the cross, and Jesus has made a public spectacle of the enemy [Col. 2:13–15]. In Jesus's name, amen.

Chapter 6

DUNAMIS POWER

As I DISCUSSED in the previous two chapters, the cross and the blood are the beginning of soul healing. But healing is not complete without the power that comes from Jesus's resurrection. Many people think all we need is the cross and to say anything more is to diminish the sacrifice Jesus made. I see their point. However, let me show you how important it is that we take possession and move in everything Jesus did for us.

On the cross our Lord broke the power of sin, sickness, the curse, and death. He also won the right for you to defeat the enemy and have eternal life. All those things and more were accomplished at Calvary. But what Jesus did on the cross does not automatically include a total healing of our souls. Why? Because when Jesus was placed in the tomb after His crucifixion, all the promises and healing He won for you were of no effect until He had risen from the dead!

The Resurrection enabled the work on the cross to be made manifest. Without it Jesus would still be dead in the tomb, and the promises He won for you would be in the grave with Him! That's why 1 Corinthians 15:17 says, "And if Christ be not raised, your faith is vain; ye are yet in your sins" (KJV).

The cross and the Resurrection go hand in hand. When Christ was crucified and raised from death, all born-again, baptized believers were there with Him to share in both victories. Romans 6:3–4 makes this truth clear.

> Or do you not know that as many of us as were baptized into Christ Jesus were baptized into His death? Therefore we were buried with Him through baptism into death, that just as Christ was raised from the dead by the glory of the Father, even so we also should walk in newness of life.

When Christ went down in death at the cross, you went down with Him, dying to sin. Likewise you have come up to new life with Him through His resurrection!

Why is this important? Countless Christians are using the cross (as they should) to battle sickness, demonic assault, and issues of every kind. However, if they stop there, they will not find total deliverance or experience the new, abundant life Christ won for us. The Bible says we went down in death at the cross but find newness of life *through the Resurrection.*

What is so vital about that? Everything! The power that comes to you from the Resurrection can totally transform every part of your life. It can heal your soul, fix your relationships, save your marriage, bring back your kids, prosper your business, and quicken your physical body. The apostle Paul acknowledged how important it is. He wrote:

> [For my determined purpose is] that I may know Him [that I may progressively become more deeply and intimately acquainted with Him, perceiving and recognizing and understanding the wonders of His Person more strongly and more clearly], and that I may in that same way come to know the power outflowing from His resurrection [which it exerts over believers].
> —PHILIPPIANS 3:10, AMPC

Here Paul lists his two highest priorities in life. Number one was to know Jesus deeply and intimately. Number two was to know the power that outflowed from His resurrection. When I read this verse, I was astounded. I totally understood Paul's giving priority to his relationship with Christ, but I had to wonder what was so amazing about this "power" from the Resurrection that knowing it came in second right after knowing Jesus. As I studied it, I was quick to see the reason behind his surprising statement.

The word "power" here is the Greek word *dynamis*. (The English spelling is *dunamis*.) When I looked it up, I saw why Paul had such interest in this power. Here are just a few meanings of the word[1]:

- Power for performing miracles

- The power and influence that belong to riches and wealth

- Excellence of soul

First, dunamis gives you the power to perform miracles. That means that because of the Resurrection, God has given you supernatural help to get breakthrough for your family, business, ministry, physical body, and any other area where you need a move of God.

Second, dunamis mantles you with the ability to have the power and influence that belong to riches and wealth. This means you have moneymaking muscle inside you because of Jesus's resurrection power. Dunamis gives every believer the ability to possess wealth and have the influence that comes with it.

Third, dunamis also gives you the power to be excellent of soul. When I read this definition, I understood even better why

Paul was so interested in getting to know this dunamis power that comes from the Resurrection. It can heal your soul! Don't forget, Paul was the guy who said he did the things he didn't want to do because of the sin nature fixed and operating in his soul. Paul had "junk in his trunk" that was negatively controlling his life. Yet the dunamis power he discovered had the ability to remedy his terrible plight!

Dunamis can transform every part of your life. It's a must-have. So how do you get it? The Bible says if you are a believer, you already have it:

> For I am not ashamed of the gospel of Christ, for it is the power [dunamis] of God to salvation for everyone who believes, for the Jew first and also for the Greek.
>
> —ROMANS 1:16

Here Paul says that dunamis is the power that brought you unto salvation. When you received Jesus as your Lord and Savior, the Holy Spirit came into you and brought dunamis with Him, which resurrected your dead spirit man unto eternal life. Right now if you're born-again, you have a tankful of dunamis inside your spirit that never runs out! This means you have 24/7 access to power that can perform miracles in your life, give you power and influence that belong to riches and wealth, and cause you to have the ability to become excellent of soul!

Stop right now and think about this. Are you sick in your body? Then command the dunamis that's already in you to flow into the place you are sick and perform a miracle. Are you broke? Release your dunamis into that situation to cause riches and wealth to manifest. Are you wounded in your soul? Command dunamis to flow out of your spirit into every unhealed area in your inner man to make it excellent so you can prosper and be in health even as your soul prospers.

Do you know that the way Jesus performed the miracles described in the Bible was through the anointing of dunamis? Acts 10:38 tells us, "God anointed Jesus of Nazareth with the Holy Spirit and with power, who went about doing good and healing all who were oppressed by the devil, for God was with Him."

Yes, the word "power" here is dunamis. Jesus did some amazing miracles, and according to this verse He used dunamis to do them. His anointing gave Him the power to perform miracles, and He used it to open blind eyes, heal the deaf and dumb, and cause the lame to walk. But dunamis also means "excellence of soul." While Jesus was working miracles, He was healing not only people's physical bodies but also their wounded souls. We know this is true because the Bible says that "great multitudes came together to hear, and to be healed by him of their *infirmities*" (Luke 5:15, KJV, emphasis added).

As mentioned previously, the word *infirmity* does not refer only to physical sickness. It's the same word used to describe the man at the pool of Siloam and the woman who was bowed over. It means "weakness, infirmity of the body, of the soul." [2]

Jesus healed people in their bodies while He was also healing them in their souls! He accomplished both things at the same time with the dunamis anointing He was carrying. In fact, I believe that when dunamis caused the people He touched to be excellent of soul, their physical bodies were healed too. They were prospered and brought into health *even as their souls prospered* (3 John 2).

Dunamis is the power that fulfills 3 John 2. Let's break it down:

I pray you may prosper [power and influence that belong to riches and wealth] in all things and be in health [power to perform miracles], just as your soul prospers [excellence of soul].

The power that makes all this come to pass in your life is dunamis! It lives in you right now. Dunamis is one of the many gifts of grace you have been given because of the finished work of Christ. You don't have to fast for it, pray for it, or beg for it. It's already yours! You just have to put what you already have to work!

We Christians are fond of quoting Ephesians 3:20, where it says that God will do "superabundantly...beyond our highest prayers, desires, thoughts, hopes, or dreams" (AMPC). It's exciting to think that God can do amazing things in our lives! But we tend to overlook the rest of the verse, which tells us that Christ causes this promise to manifest "according to the power [dunamis] that works in us."

When you put your dunamis power to work, God's superabundant blessings will be manifest in your life. This is part of laboring to enter into His rest. You must believe you already possess the power to work miracles of every kind and then labor to enter into His rest by exercising it. That's when you will see amazing demonstrations of God's power touching you and those around you.

Here are some ways to increase your faith related to the power that's available to you:

- Meditate on every dunamis and Resurrection scripture.

- Study the meanings of dunamis so you know what you have.

- Use your faith to access what's already yours.

- Use your mouth to decree it and release it into every area of your life.

It's difficult to believe that something so powerful could be living inside you. That's why you need to meditate on the scriptures about dunamis and the Resurrection. The Bible says "faith comes by hearing, and hearing by the word of God" (Rom. 10:17). As you read and meditate on all the relevant scriptures in the Bible and even in this book, your faith will grow to move in what you already have.

I have read about dunamis, talked about dunamis, and worked dunamis so much that I have high faith for it. My faith has, in turn, given me so much access to this miracle-working, soul-healing, money-making power that I am able to walk consistently in the newness of life the Resurrection promises to bring. You can too.

Once your faith accesses your dunamis, then use your mouth to release it. The Bible says, "You will...decree a thing, and it will be established for you" (Job 22:28, AMP). It also says that we can speak to a mountain, and it will move (Mark 11:23). Do you need soul healing to be established in your mind? Speak to it! Use your mouth to command the dunamis in your spirit to flow into every stronghold in your mind that is tormenting you. Are your emotions a wreck? Speak to that mountain and command it to move by the power of dunamis, and feel your peace increase!

I walk around all day decreeing I am excellent of soul. I do it in the shower, on the plane, while washing dishes, or driving to work. If I have pain in my body or am attacked by a disease, I do the same thing. I command dunamis to flow into every wound in my soul that is causing the sickness, and then

I command it to flow into my body to perform a miracle! I am constantly putting my dunamis to work so that I always experience the Ephesians 3:20 superabundant blessings of God.

Now let's look at some of the specific things dunamis can do for you.

DUNAMIS HEALS YOU OF TRAUMA

We learned in a previous chapter that trauma wounds the soul. Whether it be a stressful emotional or mental situation, an accident, a physical injury, or a sudden loss, any kind of trauma has the potential to wound your soul and cause illness as well as prevent you from fully recovering.

However, dunamis has the ability to heal every wound that comes from trauma and the illnesses that spring from it. Let's look at the example of the woman with the issue of blood. She was completely traumatized.

> And there was a woman who had had a flow of blood for twelve years, and who had endured much suffering under [the hands of] many physicians and had spent all that she had, and was no better but instead grew worse. She had heard the reports concerning Jesus, and she came up behind Him in the throng and touched His garment, for she kept saying, If I only touch His garments, I shall be restored to health.
>
> —MARK 5:25–28, AMPC

Think about everything this woman went through during her illness. She was sick for twelve years and lived as an outcast because in those days a woman who was menstruating was considered unclean. She also spent all the money she had on many different doctors, but instead of healing her, they only brought her more suffering. In fact, instead of getting better, she grew worse.

What did Jesus do about it? He healed her with the dunamis power God anointed Him with! When she touched the hem of His garment, "Immediately the fountain of her blood was dried up, and she felt in her body that she was healed of the affliction. And Jesus, immediately knowing in Himself that power [dunamis] had gone out of Him, turned around in the crowd and said, 'Who touched My clothes?'" (Mark 5:29–30).

Jesus felt the dunamis release from Him when that woman touched His garments. As a reminder, dunamis means "excellence of soul" as well as "power for performing miracles," so we know the Lord healed her in both her body and her soul. When she touched the hem of His garment, dunamis flowed into her whole being, which first healed her soul of every trauma she had lived through and then performed a miracle in her body. She prospered in her health even as her soul was prospered.

About five years ago I was in a car accident. My media director, our driver, and I were headed down a highway to a meeting when another vehicle crossed the road right in front of us. Going highway speed, we T-boned the other car, crashing headfirst into its side.

Sitting in the back bench, I was thrown violently against the seat in front of me. Instantly I realized I couldn't breathe. At first I thought I had just gotten the wind knocked out of me, but it was much worse than that. I later learned that I had broken two ribs and was suffering from a hemothorax, which means my lungs were filling up with fluid and blood.

Everyone kept asking me if I was OK, but I couldn't speak. The suitcases were flung all over the back seat, and the door on my side was smashed shut, so the paramedics had to drag me out the other door. By this point I was in a total panic. There is nothing worse than not being able to breathe. It feels as if you are drowning. It was one of the most frightening things I have ever lived through.

Even after the paramedics put an oxygen mask on me and loaded me into the ambulance, I was still unable to speak. But that didn't stop me from praying for my life. While the blood and fluid continued to fill my lungs, I began to say in my mind, "I have an endless supply of dunamis. I have a tankful. I am excellent of soul. I am healed of this trauma. I am prospered and brought into health even as my soul prospers."

On the outside I was struggling violently to live, but inside I was focused on walking in the truth I knew could save me. We arrived at the hospital to discover that it was the worst night they had experienced in years. The emergency room was full of accident victims, shootings, and overdoses. They took me for an MRI and then parked my gurney right outside the door to surgery. There I lay, fighting for oxygen. Tears of pain, fear, and frustration flowed down my face as I waited for help. All the while I continued to pray and put my dunamis to work.

They finally wheeled me into surgery. The plan was to drill a hole in my chest and suck out of the blood and fluid that was filling my lungs. But God had a different plan. Right as they rolled me through the doors, I suddenly could take in a huge breath. It was so loud the people outside in the hall heard it, and I began talking for the first time since the accident.

The bleeding had mysteriously stopped, and I could breathe in and out easily. It was totally amazing! Even the excruciating pain I had in my body from the hemothorax was gone. I knew I had experienced a miracle. My soul had been healed of the trauma from the accident, and my body had followed suit.

Dunamis had saved my life. But what was strange was that I still had two broken ribs. A few weeks later I was at home trying to recover, but the pain from the broken ribs was excruciating. That's when I asked my intercessors to come over and pray for dunamis to perform a miracle in my body. After we worshipped for an hour, I was still in agony, but then that night the power kicked in.

I dreamed that a woman was painting the wall in front of me. All night this went on. In the morning right as I woke up, she finished the piece. It was a picture of a waterfall. Jesus said that river of living water, dunamis, would flow continuously from our innermost being. At that moment all my pain left, and I knew my ribs were healed. I was so sure, I went to the doctor and insisted on getting an X-ray, even though two separate MRIs had already confirmed I had two broken ribs. When it was processed, the doctor said it looked as though I had never broken my ribs in the first place. Again, dunamis to the rescue.

Have you ever gone through a trauma, or are you going through one right now? Start releasing dunamis into your soul to make it excellent and into your body to heal you. Put your dunamis to work, and expect a miracle!

DUNAMIS ENDS DEMONIC ASSAULTS

The Bible says that Jesus made a public spectacle of the enemy at the cross. Yet it isn't only His blood that causes the enemy to flee. Dunamis does too.

Let's look again at Acts 10:38:

> God anointed Jesus of Nazareth with the Holy Spirit and with power [dunamis], who went about doing good and healing all who were oppressed by the devil, for God was with Him.

This verse says that Jesus used His anointing of dunamis to heal all who were oppressed by the devil! How does that work? When dunamis is released into your soul, it makes it excellent and strengthens and reinforces it. As your soul becomes whole, then you can resist any demonic strongman. Don't forget the scripture Matthew 12:29: "Or else how can one enter into a strong man's house, and spoil his goods, except he first bind the strong man? and then he will spoil his house" (KJV).

Again, one meaning of the word *strongman* is "one who has strength of soul to sustain the attacks of Satan, strong and therefore exhibiting many excellences."[3]

The way you bind the strongman—the enemy—is by becoming a strongman yourself—one who is strong in soul. Dunamis fulfills this scripture in Matthew 12. It is the power that causes you to become so excellent in your soul that you will have nothing in you that is in common with Satan so he will have no power over you.

The strongman gets his legal right to attack you through wounds in your soul, but when you are healed, he will have no power to afflict you. Jesus confirms this is true in a powerful statement recorded in John 14:

> I will not talk with you much more, for the prince (evil genius, ruler) of the world is coming. And he has no claim on Me. [He has nothing in common with Me; there is nothing in Me that belongs to him, and he has no power over Me.]
>
> —JOHN 14:30, AMPC

Here, Jesus gives us the key to supernatural authority over the enemy. If you don't have anything in your soul that is in common with Satan, then he will have no power over you!

That's how dunamis can defeat the devil. It makes you excellent of soul.

Are you battling with a demonic force? There is a high probability you have something in your soul that is in common with that spirit, allowing it to attack you. No matter how much you bind and rebuke it, it will not leave because it has a legal right to be there as long as your soul is wounded. Often the wound is from habitual sin. If this is the case, you must repent in order for the spirit to loose its hold on you, as you will see in the next section. Then release the dunamis power that is in you into every unhealed area of your soul that the enemy is using as a legal right to attack you.

We need to change the way we make war. Stop screaming at the enemy and rebuking him. Instead, release dunamis into your inner man first. Command it to go to every place in your soul that needs strengthening. Decree that your soul is becoming excellent by the power of dunamis so you have nothing in you that is in common with Satan. Once you are healed, then bind the strongman and ransack his house. While doing this don't forget that you have the same anointing as Jesus, who used dunamis to heal all who were oppressed by the devil.

DUNAMIS HELPS YOU STOP SINNING

Have you ever been stuck in a sinful behavior, and no matter how much you repented, it still seemed to control you? Is there something you are doing now that you know you shouldn't be doing but can't seem to stop? If so, you are in good company. As I mentioned earlier, the apostle Paul had the same problem.

> Now if I do what I do not desire to do, it is no longer I
> doing it [it is not myself that acts], but the sin [principle]
> which dwells within me [fixed and operating in my soul].
> —ROMANS 7:20, AMPC

If you're stuck in sin, don't let the enemy or your conscience make you feel condemned. Just do what Paul did. He relied on dunamis to heal his inner man and asked that God would help others do the same. In Ephesians 3 Paul prayed for dunamis to heal our souls.

> May He grant you out of the rich treasury of His glory
> to be strengthened and reinforced with mighty power in
> the inner man.
> —EPHESIANS 3:16, AMPC

Paul put dunamis to work by praying for our souls to be strengthened and reinforced by its mighty power! Remember that Paul said he wanted to know the power of Christ's resurrection. I am sure the same prayer he prayed for us he also prayed for himself to help him stop doing the things he didn't want to do.

If you're trapped in something that has you in its grip, first repent. Then pray Paul's prayer over yourself every day until it breaks. As you continue to release dunamis through this prayer, your soul will be strengthened, reinforced, and built up to totally resist any temptation.

DUNAMIS HEALS YOUR MIND

One thing that believers sometimes have to overcome is strongholds in their minds. A *stronghold* is a fortress of thoughts that has been created in your mind because of a habitual pattern of thinking that is not in line with God's Word. It can cause you to embrace wrong, harmful, and even dangerous ideas and doctrines that devastate your life. For example, let's say you were once in a bad car accident, as I was. Because of your experience, you worry every time you get in a car that you will be in a wreck. Over time this thought becomes so persistent that it creates a stronghold of fear in your mind—one that controls you to the point of making you not want to get into a car at all. This stronghold is in direct opposition to the many commands in Scripture to "fear not" and the verse in Philippians 4:6 to "be anxious for nothing," yet you can't seem to shake it.

Thankfully there is a remedy, as we have already seen. Second Corinthians 10:4–5 (KJV) tells us:

> (For the weapons of our warfare are not carnal, but mighty through God to the pulling down of strong holds;) casting down imaginations, and every high thing that exalteth itself against the knowledge of God, and bringing into captivity every thought to the obedience of Christ.

According to this verse, God has given us mighty weapons to cast down strongholds. The word "mighty" here is the Greek word *dynatos* (related to dunamis), and it means "strong in soul."[4] This means the weapons of your warfare for demolishing strongholds are the cross, the blood of Jesus Christ, and His dunamis power because they all heal the soul.

Sometimes the strongholds in our minds are so ingrained we don't recognize them. When I spend time in worship, I ask God to search my heart and mind to see if I have any erroneous thinking that I am mistakenly agreeing with. I wash my mind in Jesus's blood and command dunamis power to flow into every thought that doesn't line up with the will of God. This would be a good habit for you to develop as well.

Also, start paying attention to what you are letting yourself think about. The more you allow your brain to focus on an offense or a worry, the more strongholds will build up in your mind that will have the power to bring sickness and devastation to your life. If you catch yourself thinking something negative or harmful, immediately attack it with your mighty weapons! Repent for that thought and command dunamis to flow into your mind to make you excellent in this area of your soul.

DUNAMIS EMPOWERS YOU TO PROSPER FINANCIALLY

As we discussed before, 3 John 2 says that you will prosper even as your soul prospers. The prosperity this verse refers to doesn't include just spiritual well-being or the health of relationships. It also includes financial increase. Again, the meaning of the word "prosper"—*euodoō*—is "to succeed in business affairs."[5] God wants you to prosper in all your financial endeavors, but it will only happen as your soul prospers.

That's where dunamis comes in. It makes you excellent of soul, and afterward your blessings will explode because God can trust you to steward the increase well.

Once your soul is healed, dunamis will cause you to walk in the power and influence that belong to riches and wealth. Have you ever noticed how much authority, power, and influence wealthy people have? One person who possesses wealth can literally change the world, as many philanthropists have done through the years.

The kind of influence they have is the kind God wants to give Christians, and He is going to use the resurrection, dunamis power of His Son to make that happen. I'm thankful that I have this power working for me personally and in my ministry. I not only walk in prosperity because of the healed condition of my soul, but I also have influence. When I receive a vision from the Lord and share it corporately with the body of Christ, large numbers of people get behind me to support and execute it. Then collectively as a body we make things happen that positively affect people around the world.

A good example is our prison outreach, Expected End Ministries. As long as I can remember, prison ministry has never been "cool." It was always the last outreach people would sign up for and the last one to receive funding. Many years ago the Lord told me I would change the public's mind about prison outreach and the prisoners we serve. The consensus has gone from "Leave those criminals in there; they deserve what they got" to "Let's serve, heal, and free God's captive people!"

Currently we are changing the face of more than three thousand prisons around the world, and that number is rapidly rising. Through media, a massive book campaign in which we have given away nearly four hundred thousand free copies of my books, and miracle healing tours, we have made prison ministry one of the most sought-after mission fields in the world. People now understand that they don't have to travel across the planet to do missions. Rather they can pray, financially support, and even travel with us to their nearest prison and see the hand of God do the impossible. That's influence that belongs to riches and wealth. That's dunamis in action.

I didn't start out that way; I was just as wounded and broke as the rest of the world. Because I was previously a meth cook, drug dealer, and "collector," I had a lot of wounds in my soul that were connected to money. Yet as I was rapidly becoming the leader of an international ministry that would eventually handle millions of dollars a year in giving, I knew I needed to be healed. Thank God for dunamis.

In the very beginning of the ministry, we were broke and in major debt. All our credit cards were maxed out, and the debt was growing with interest. We needed more than $21,000 just to get out of the hole, an amount that at the time seemed impossible to acquire.

One Saturday I was on my way to conduct a meeting. That morning I asked God for help. While I worshipped, I prayed for my soul to be healed, and God took me into a deep sleep. I saw a vision of a shiny new black brassiere. Startled, I came out of the sleep saying, "God, what does that mean?" I immediately started thinking about it and realized that when a business is running in the black, it is at break-even or above from a financial perspective. Then I thought about what a brassiere could possibly represent. In the natural it supplies support for a woman whose breasts feed and nourish babies. The one I saw was brand-new. As I rolled these things around in my mind, I heard the Lord say, "I just healed your soul, so now I can bring you a new source of support that will cause you to be in the black and enable you to feed your spiritual children!"

What God promised was fulfilled just hours later in the meeting. A new supporter gave us a large donation, and between that and the offering we brought in, the entire debt of $21,000 was wiped out. Soul healing had caused us to operate in the black!

Right now you have power in you to become excellent of soul so you can prosper and receive the power and influence that come with riches and wealth—and so you can change and influence your world. But you need to put it to work. Do you have a financial need? First ask God to heal your soul of anything that is blocking your increase. Then release the power and influence for riches and wealth that's inside you into that situation, and get ready to receive new ideas, investment strategies, and business and ministry ventures, as well as new, creative inventions.

DUNAMIS HEALS GENERATIONAL WOUNDS FROM THE WOMB

In a previous chapter we talked about the fact that soul wounds can come from generational iniquities and be passed down to you while you are being formed in the womb. The good news is that dunamis is so powerful it can heal you of these generational iniquities and the birth defects that come from them.

Let me prove it through the story in Acts of the man who was born lame from birth. Don't forget that Peter called this man "impotent," referring to the state of his soul. So he was born with a soul wound that made his physical body lame.

After Peter and John healed the man, Peter told everyone how they did it. He said to the excited onlookers: "Ye men of Israel, why marvel ye at this? or why look ye so earnestly on us, as though by our own power or holiness we had made this man to walk?" (Acts 3:12, KJV).

The word "power" in this verse is the word dunamis. Here Peter is saying, "Look, it wasn't by my own ability that this man was healed; it was by the dunamis power of the Lord Jesus Christ." So it was dunamis that healed that man of not only the wound he received while in the womb but also the physical disease that came from it.

PRAYER ACTIVATION

Let's close this chapter by putting our dunamis to work. Pray the following soul-healing prayer with me.

Lord Jesus, the Bible says that when I was born again, the Holy Spirit came into me and brought dunamis with Him. Now I decree that I have a tankful of power that never runs out and that causes me to be able to perform miracles, gives me the power and influence that comes with riches and wealth, and makes me excellent of soul. I put the dunamis that is in me to work right now so I can have above and beyond anything that I could ever ask or imagine. I command dunamis to heal me of all the effects of trauma in my soul and in my body. I decree that dunamis is healing me of everything I have in my soul that is in common with Satan so he will have no power over me. I pray as Paul prayed that I would be strengthened and reinforced with the mighty power of dunamis in my inner man so I can resist all sin. I release my mighty weapon of dunamis so my soul can become strong and I can break every stronghold in my mind. And I decree that my soul is prospered by dunamis so I can prosper in my finances and gain the power and influence that come with riches and wealth. In Jesus's name, amen.

Chapter 7

PREMATURE DEATH AND BONE DISEASE

I HAD BEEN IN prison for only a few years when my parents filed an appeal with the federal court to shorten my prison time. The probability of winning was only .05 percent, but they felt prompted by God to do it.

At the time I was in a large federal prison in California, where the Lord led me and a few other women to start a Christian group with prayer circles, worship, and Bible studies. We grew in numbers quickly, and God started moving among us, doing miracles of all kinds.

Then the Lord brought about a big transition in my life. Right after I first lost in court and was sentenced to twelve years in prison, I received a prophecy that the chemicals in the lab where I was busted would eventually be destroyed. When I heard it, I thought it couldn't happen because I had already been sentenced according to that evidence. But then God dramatically increased my faith by giving me a new out date. One night in my cell He said I would be getting out on November 21, 2003—seven years before my release date. It seemed impossible, but then the court suddenly allowed the appeal my parents had filed to be heard!

The prosecuting attorney responded by saying he was going to weigh all the chemicals in order to give me even more time. Yet when he went down to the evidence locker to do so, everything was gone. The chemicals had been destroyed because of their dangerous nature. When the court calculated my new out date, it was November 21, 2003. Both of God's words had come to pass! (You can read all the details of my arrest, imprisonment, and miraculous release in my book *The Captivity Series: The Key to Your Expected End*.)

Triumphantly I went home. However, waiting for me was a black cloud that had been over my family for twenty-five years: my mother's deteriorating physical condition.

FROM BAD TO WORSE

In the early 1980s a tick had bitten mom while she was taking a walk. It released a spirochete bacterium into her system that caused her to develop Lyme disease.[1] A few years later she developed severe rheumatoid arthritis, which—when coupled with the Lyme—began to consume her bones and cartilage.

First, she lost both knees, and doctors put in artificial replacements. Then the cartilage inside the knucklebones of her hands were destroyed, which caused the little bones in her fingers to fall out of the knuckle sockets. Since there was nothing to secure the bones in place, she could literally take hold of her fingers and spin them around.

Several years later her left hip became so deteriorated it was removed, and an artificial hip was surgically implanted. Shortly after that she collapsed and was rushed to the hospital. When the surgeon reopened the incision, he discovered the Lyme disease had eaten the plastic parts of the man-made hip! It was so bad they had to break her thighbone in order to get the device out. From that point on, her leg flopped helplessly around from side to side because it was no longer anchored to her body. To make light of the situation, we started calling her the "boneless chicken."

If that wasn't enough, the other side of Mom's pelvic bone became so weakened that the doctors wanted to take it out too because they feared it would cause further damage. It was a nightmare. Plus, at one point Mom could no longer lift her arms, so she had X-rays of her shoulders taken. The results showed that her bones looked like Swiss cheese—each of them were riddled with holes.

The pain that accompanied this "consuming" of her bones was excruciating, even with the strongest painkillers. Through it she and my stepdad kept their faith, though there were many times that in the middle of a pain attack her prayers would turn into screams. My parents incessantly sought out new medical avenues to provide relief, but they finally lost count after they had consulted more than sixty doctors.

SEARCHING FOR AN ANSWER

After I was released from prison, I lived with Mom and Dad off and on for a few years. It was devastating for me to watch Mom struggle to eat or pick up things, see her deformed body bedridden and deteriorating year after year, and hear her endless screaming from the agonizing pain. I felt driven to pray for her as I had never prayed for any person or situation in my life. I was determined to find a supernatural answer to her plague.

I coupled my prayers with a great deal of fasting. In fact, fasting became a way of life for me. I would finish one fast only to begin another a few days later. I would worship and pray for hours and hours at a time. I dug into the Scriptures, tenaciously looking for answers, direction, and hope. Day and night I waited in desperation, listening for God to show me a path to Mom's victory. For a few years nothing happened; then one day I got a breakthrough.

Through a series of providential circumstances God led me to visit Bethel Church in Redding, California, where amazing miracles were happening. While I was there, two women laid hands on me, and when they did, I sensed power flow into me. It felt as if warm oil was being poured over my head and down into my body. It was so tangible my arm felt too heavy to lift.

When I got back home, I rushed to tell my family everything that had happened and then laid hands on my mom. Suddenly I discovered that I had a supernatural "switch" inside me. Whenever I touched her or anyone else, divine power and heat were released from my body.

Supernatural Healings

I immediately experienced fruit from my prayers. First, my stepdad was healed of a serious issue that was going to require surgery. Then my mom was set free from a twenty-year-long addiction to Dilaudid, the prescription equivalent to heroin. Then Mom's remaining hip started causing her more pain and problems because the thighbone kept popping in and out of the hip socket. One day I got a word from God to command it to go into place. When I did, Mom said, "Ouch" and then described what she felt was similar to what happens when the ball on a truck pops into the hitch of a trailer. After that she never had problems with that hip again.

Eventually God told me that Mom was going to die but that He would resurrect her in answer to my prayers. On the exact day He said the event would occur, she went into a coma, and her breathing became extremely fast and shallow. The doctors said she had only hours left, but I knew better. I commanded the spirit of death to leave and felt a wave of power as it did. Mom woke up an hour later and said she had a dream she had died. I told her she had but that God had brought her back to me.

The miracle was exciting, but in the end it wasn't enough. Three months later mom passed away for good. I wasn't there, and by the time I arrived, she was being taken to the funeral home. Every day for three days I had the caretakers bring her out of the refrigerator so I could pray for her to come back. What I didn't realize until later was that once she saw the glory of God and her eternal home, she didn't want to return. After all she had been through, I wouldn't have come back either.

EFFECT OF A WOUNDED SOUL

What caused such a vicious illness to consume and destroy my mother's life? After she died, I was given her Bible. I was shocked to find she had underlined many soul scriptures. The Holy Spirit was trying to tell her that it was her wounded soul that was the culprit. However, she obviously didn't understand, and I didn't either—until later. By then it was too late to save Mom, but since then hundreds of thousands of people have been transformed through this truth.

I believe my mom died before her time because of wounds in her soul that caused her to get sick. An unhealed soul can bring all sorts of diseases on people and cause them to die before God's intended time. Job 14:5 tells us that all men have an appointed time to pass away: "Since a man's days are already determined, and the number of his months is wholly in Your control, and he cannot pass the bounds of his allotted time" (AMPC).

God has appointed the number of our days and also the specific moment when each one of us will pass into glory. However, many people are dying out of God's time. I know this is true because if it weren't, the Lord would not have raised anyone from death. Think about it. While on earth Jesus resurrected three people, yet what did He say? "The Son can do nothing of Himself, but what He sees the Father do" (John 5:19). Jesus only did what He saw the Father doing, so He would have never raised someone who died at God's appointed time. Doing so would have gone against God's will.

Jesus resurrected Lazarus, so it must not have been his time to die (John 11). Because He raised Jairus's daughter from death, it must not have been her time (Matt. 9:18–26). And the same goes for the widow of Nain's son (Luke 7:11–17).

Does the Bible tell us what caused these people to get sick and pass before their appointed day? In the case of Lazarus, I believe Scripture indictates he had a soul wound that caused him to get sick and die prior to his intended day. Let's look at some proof.

> Now a certain man was sick, named Lazarus, of Bethany, the town of Mary and her sister Martha. (It was that Mary which anointed the Lord with ointment and wiped his feet with her hair whose brother Lazarus was sick.) Therefore his sisters sent unto him, saying, Lord, behold, he whom thou lovest is sick. When Jesus heard that, he said, This sickness is not unto death, but for the glory of God, that the Son of God might be glorified thereby.
> —JOHN 11:1–4, KJV

After Jesus heard that Lazarus was sick, He declared, "This sickness is not unto death" (v. 4). The direct translation of the word "sickness" in Greek is *astheneia*. It's the exact same word as the word "infirmity," which means "weakness" and "infirmity of the body...of the soul."[2] So according to Jesus, Lazarus had an unhealed area in his soul that caused him to get physically sick and die before his appointed day.

Bitterness Causes Premature Death

It's amazing to me how many people believe God puts sickness on us to teach us a lesson and that He sends Satan against us to discipline us. How could God make us sick when His Son gave His very life to heal every disease and break every curse? By His stripes we are healed! (Isa. 53:5). The Bible says Jesus came to destroy the works of the enemy (1 John 3:8) and take away the power of the one who held the power of death, which is the devil (Heb. 2:14), and that He made a public spectacle of Satan at the cross (Col. 2:15). So there is no way God would go against what His Son gave His very life to accomplish by giving Satan permission to assault us.

It is never the will of God that we die of sickness and disease. But our inner man allows sickness and Satan to take us before our time. Look at this revealing scripture from Job:

> One dieth in his full strength, being wholly at ease and quiet. His breasts are full of milk, and his bones are moistened with marrow. And another dieth in the bitterness of his soul.
>
> —Job 21:23–24, KJV

Did you see the difference between the way the two different types of men Job described will die? The first one passes in peace. His strength is unabated. He is disease-free, and his bones are full of marrow and moistening. This is a beautiful description of God's will for all men as they pass on to glory. We have an appointed time to die, and when that day comes, God wants us to be strong, with healthy bones and a disease-free body. We should be so fit that we are running marathons, chasing our grandchildren around, being active with our family and friends, and having no illness at all. Then, when your appointed day comes, you lie down, and poof! You're gone. Your family finds you on your bed with a big smile on your face. That's the will of God for the passing of all His people.

However, that is not happening to a majority of people in this world, even believers. Why not? According to Job, the other type of man described in Job 21:23–24 dies in "bitterness of his soul." People are dying out of their appointed time of diseases and disorders because they have wounds in their souls that are allowing them to get sick. Job pointed out that it is the sin of bitterness that causes some people to die horribly. We will talk more about bitterness in this chapter and later in the book.

When someone dies of a hideous disease, you sometimes hear people saying, "Well, it must have been his time." I violently disagree. If someone is dying of a disease, it is not his time. According to the Bible, all God's people are supposed to die in full strength with our bones filled with marrow and moistening! If a person is not healthy when he dies, that is an indicator that he is passing away before his time because his soul is wounded. That's when you can fight for that person's life with the blood of Jesus Christ and His dunamis power.

I believe my mom died before her appointed time from soul wounds that made her physically ill. Her bones weren't filled with moistening and marrow, so she did not pass like the first man described in Job. Instead, she died in bitterness of her soul.

BITTERNESS AFFECTS THE BONES

Bone issues can be the result of a wounded soul. A very simple example is the woman bowed over from a spirit of infirmity who had her bones bent for eighteen years (Luke 13:11). Again, the word *infirmity* means "weakness and infirmity of the body, of the soul."[3] She had a wound in her soul, and that's what was allowing a spirit to literally wreak havoc on her skeletal system.

Healthy bones and bone marrow are crucial to good health. Marrow is responsible for keeping your whole body well. When disease affects bone marrow, it can no longer function effectively, and deadly ailments can be the result.

According to the scripture in Job 21 quoted previously, bitterness can wound the soul and have a negative impact on our bone marrow, which, in turn, can have devastating effects on the body. Mom's bones were literally eaten away, which is what bitterness does. It consumes you.

Bitterness can run in your family and be passed down to you while you are being formed in the womb. (We'll talk more about this in the chapter on character bents.) It ran in my family. My grandmother was the most amazing woman. I could sit with her for hours listening to her stories and enlightening wisdom. Yet there were times when the bitterness in her soul would rise up and manifest in many ways, including severe cupboard door slamming.

Mom was the same. In my view she was the funniest, toughest, and most clever, educated, and talented person on the planet. Hanging out with her always left me feeling more in love with her than the day before. Yet she often spoke with intensity of the many painful things she had lived through that had left her bitter. There were also certain people she just could not forgive. She said she did, but her words concerning them betrayed her. I believe Mom's bitterness played a part in wounding her soul and causing her freaky bone disorder. Her bones had no marrow and moistening, and she died before her time of bitterness of her soul.

I followed in both Grandma's and Mom's footsteps but on

a level that made them look like Mary Poppins. My bitterness was so fierce that it was terrifying to those around me and even to me. It almost killed me through endless street wars and three bouts with cancer, along with many other afflictions. Thank God I understood this revelation because when I was healed of bitterness, I was also healed physically—without having to go through the horror of chemotherapy or radiation.

The Remedy for Bitterness

How do you heal a bitter soul? The blood from the cross and Resurrection, and dunamis power. The blood is your remedy for the sin of bitterness. When I felt it rise up in my soul, I battled with the blood and the finished work of Christ. I labored to enter into His rest by releasing the blood to cleanse my soul, and then I commanded dunamis to flow into my mind and emotions so I could become excellent in every area in which I had been bitter.

As I have repeatedly gone through this process, I have experienced a major shift. I feel so much peace now! I also have a new level of self-control that prevents me from exploding and becoming angry. I am not perfect, and I still have my moments, but they are few and far between and are in no way violent.

Dunamis power is what Jesus used to bring His friend Lazarus back from the dead. Don't forget that the apostle Paul said dunamis is "resurrection power." He prayed to "know Him and the power [dunamis] of His resurrection" (Phil. 3:10).

Dunamis is the power that flows out of the resurrection of Christ. Acts 10:38 says Jesus was anointed with this resurrection power, and He used it to raise Lazarus from the tomb (John 11:43). What did this power do for Lazarus? First, it caused his spirit to return into his earthly shell so he could come back to life (v. 44). Then dunamis healed his body of four days of rotting in the grave. Dunamis means "the power for performing miracles,"[4] and that's what Lazarus needed. His thirty trillion cells were dead, as were his brain, organs, skin, blood, and the rest of his mortal body.[5] When Jesus released dunamis resurrection power on him, it performed a miracle, and every part of his body was restored.

Yet, that is not all that dunamis resurrection power did that day. Dunamis also means "excellence of soul,"[6] so it also healed Lazarus of the wounds in his soul that caused him to get sick and die in the first place!

People are dying out of their appointed time because unhealed areas in their souls are causing them to get sick. I believe this is exactly what happened to my mom and what is also happening to millions of people around the world right now.

HARVEST OF MIRACLES

When Mom died, the Lord told me that she was my "seed." The Bible says unless a seed falls into the ground and dies, it cannot produce a harvest (John 12:24). The harvest I have reaped in bone miracles has been so massive I could never have imagined it! I may not have understood the revelation of the soul in time to heal Mom's bones, but I have seen thousands of healings manifest since her passing as a result of this teaching.

One woman who was healed in my meeting had fallen from a second floor down an icy stairway and broken her spine in several places. She had also broken her left hip and two ribs. As a result of her accident, she had her spine fused, and the procedure produced a pinched sciatic nerve. Along with other issues she was dealing with, these conditions created tremendous pain.

At the time she came to the meeting, she was miserable and had been in an even greater amount of pain than usual that day. And she wasn't looking forward to having to sit in the chairs at the meeting because they would make the pain much worse.

Though she came to the meeting, she left after a while, intending to go home. But she felt compelled to stay. When she returned to the meeting, we were still in the praise-and-worship portion of the event, and she heard me pronounce a word from the Lord: "Backs are being healed right now."

She said she reached her arms out to God to soak in His presence during the worship when she heard a terrible sound, as if the ceiling above her was breaking. She said it sounded as if there had been a terrible crash, but nobody else seemed to hear it. Then suddenly she realized all the pain was completely gone from her back. First she bent down, and then she squatted on the floor—things she hadn't been able to do in decades—and there was no pain. She was completely healed that night—not only of the physical problems in her bones but also of the issues in her soul from the trauma she had experienced for more than two decades.

I have seen thousands of bone miracles in people of all ages. An inmate in one of our meetings reported that he had fallen down twice when coming out of the chow hall. The first time, he fractured his tailbone. The second time, he broke it. On top of that, his hips were deteriorating. The doctor was going to put a cast on him that started at his hips and went up to his chest. However, it wasn't flexible enough for him to wear, so he was left without any support at all. The pain in his body was so bad he couldn't get out of bed in the morning. Once he even fell while trying to get up. During the meeting he said the soul healing prayers numerous times, and the next morning he had no trouble getting up. In fact, he said he felt as if he were a teenager again. He had absolutely no pain and could walk easily for the first time in years.

Another woman had broken her back, shattered her tail-bone, and dislocated a disk, which she could feel protruding out of her back. When she walked, she experienced a lot of pain—she could actually feel the bone grinding against the other bones. After worship I got a word of knowledge about a back being healed, and she started feeling stuff move around.

The next day she noticed the disk was no longer bulging out of her back, and all her pain was gone. Then she tried to do things she couldn't do before and was able to accomplish them without pain or resistance. She was so impressed with what God had done, she showed her friends she had been healed by doing a dead drop on her tailbone—and it didn't even hurt!

PRAYER ACTIVATION

If you're like me, you've been through some hard-core situations, and they left you feeling bitter and angry. You have also probably dealt with some really difficult people and become bitter because of it. You'll know this is true if you catch yourself replaying painful incidents over and over in your mind or replaying the hurtful words people said to you. You will also know you're bitter if you catch yourself rehearsing what you'd say to a person who has hurt you while telling him off. When your mind is consumed with bitterness, it will wound your soul and then eat away at every part of your being, including your bones.

Repeat these decrees and prayers with me.

Lord, I repent for any bitterness that is in my soul.
I ask for forgiveness for being angry and offended.
I repent for exhibiting strong animosity and

bitterness toward my friends, family, foes, bosses, leaders, spouse, children, and anyone else in my life. Take Your blood, Jesus, and wash me clean of this sin. I decree that the blood is cleansing me and that I am already forgiven because of what Jesus did on the cross.

I also repent for being overcome by bitter grief, anguish, or disappointment because of all the traumatic events I have lived through. I repent for showing bitter resentment toward people or situations. Wash away my sin of bitterness right now by Your blood. I repent for becoming bitter about difficult relationships. I repent for saying bitter, sarcastic words and cutting remarks toward anyone. In the name of Jesus, I repent for being intolerable, unbearable, harsh, and corrosive in my tone and for making sharp comments, throwing fits, and being unpleasant and disagreeable because I was bitter.

I also forgive everyone who acted the same to me because they were bitter.

Now I thank You, Lord, for your dunamis power that comes from the Resurrection. I decree that it is healing the wounds in me that came from my sins of bitterness and is causing me to be excellent of soul. I decree right now that I am being set free from bitterness and all the negative thoughts, words, and actions that go along with it. I decree that I am excellent of soul.

I also decree that anything in my soul that might make me sick and pass on before my time is being healed right now by Your finished work on the cross and dunamis Resurrection power. I am like

Lazarus. This sickness will not end in death but for the glory of the Lord! In Jesus's name, amen.

Now say these commands over yourself:

I command any spirit of infirmity that is on me to leave now in Jesus's name. I no longer have anything in my soul that is in common with it, so it has to go. I also command my bones and marrow to be healed, pain to be gone, cartilage to be restored, and joints to be healed. I am pain-free right now. I command my body to come into alignment and every part of my spine to be healed and restored. I release creative miracles into my body through the dunamis power that's in me, and I decree that my bones are full of marrow and moistening. In the name of Jesus, amen.

Now if you had some sort of a bone issue, check it out right now. Move around for a few minutes and then try to do something you couldn't do before. If you are still not healed, continue decreeing soul-healing prayers over yourself, and expect your miracle.

Chapter 8

WHAT IS STOPPING THE FLOW?

EVERY BELIEVER HAS been given a full tank of dunamis power, which includes the power to perform miracles, have influence to gain riches and wealth, and produce excellence of soul. The Word promises that each one of us will experience even greater things than we can think, ask, or imagine (Eph. 3:20). Why, then, are so many Christians still sick, broke, and in a mess?

The answer is that sometimes there are blocks in the soul that are preventing the flow of dunamis power from going where it is needed. When these hindrances are removed by faith in the finished work of Christ and His blood, then believers will experience the fulfillment of Jesus's words:

> He who believes in Me [who cleaves to and trusts in and relies on Me] as the Scripture has said, From his innermost being shall flow [continuously] springs and rivers of living water.
>
> —JOHN 7:38, AMPC

Jesus said that springs and even rivers of living water will flow continuously from our innermost beings. These rivers are the dunamis power that's in our spirit man. The proof is in the word "living," in Greek *zaō*, which means "having vital power in itself and exerting the same upon the soul."[1] These living waters Jesus talked about have soul-healing ability, so their source must be dunamis because they make you excellent of soul.

Jesus promises that dunamis will flow *continuously* from your spirit man. However, if that were the case, you would constantly be getting healed in both your soul and your body—and this is not our daily reality. We still act out and suffer from physical issues because we are wounded.

ANCIENT GATES

So what's up? Is Jesus a liar? Certainly not. The problem is that something in us is stopping the flow. I believe there are gates and doors in our souls and bodies that are shut down, preventing dunamis from flowing out of our spirit man into our souls and then into our mortal bodies to perform miracles. These gates and doors can be compared to those mentioned in Psalm 24:7–9 (AMP):

> Lift up your heads, O gates, and be lifted up, ancient doors, that the King of glory may come in. Who is this King of glory? The LORD strong and mighty, the LORD mighty in battle. Lift up your heads, O gates, and lift them up, you ancient doors, that the King of glory may come in. Who is…this King of glory? The LORD of hosts, He is the King of glory.

This scripture repeatedly commands the ancient gates and doors to be lifted up. What is it referring to? The words "gates" (Hebrew *shaar*) and "doors" (Hebrew *pethach*) refer to the openings and entryways in a temple.[2] In ancient times the temple was a building, but the Bible says that now *you* are the temple of the Lord:

> Or do you not know that your body is the temple of the
> Holy Spirit who is in you, whom you have from God,
> and you are not your own?
>
> —1 CORINTHIANS 6:19

THE GATES IN US

You are the temple of God, and inside you are ancient gates and doors just as there were in the physical temple in biblical times. These doorways need to be "lifted up" in a spiritual sense because they are preventing the King of glory from coming in and healing every part of your being.

So what are these gates? You have five of them in your body: an eye gate, through which images enter; an ear gate, through which sounds and words enter; a mouth gate, which allows you to take in nourishment and also to speak; a nose gate, one of your most important sensory gates and the one through which smells enter; and the gateway of touch and physical sensations.

In addition to the body gates you also have doorways to your inner man. These lead to your subconscious and conscious mind, your imagination, your reasoning and intellect, your memories, your will, and your emotions. If you look up the word "gate" (*shaar*) in Hebrew, you will find that its prime root means to "reason out, calculate, reckon, estimate."[3] Where do you reason and calculate? In your mind, which is part of your soul.

There are gates in the realm of your soul that give access to every part of your inner man. If any of them are closed down, then the rivers of living water that are supposed to flow continuously from your spirit will not be able to penetrate into your soul to make you excellent and then go into your body to quicken it.

We can compare the gates in our souls to those in a water dam. Every dam has gates in it that regulate the flow of water going through. When those gates are shut, the water can't run, and the flow dries up. It's the same with the living rivers inside you. If the doors are shut, those restorative rivers can't pour into the places you need healing. This is why Psalm 24 tells us to command our ancient gates to be lifted up so the King of glory and His dunamis power can come in.

How the Gates Become Closed

What causes these gates and doors to close? Soul wounds caused by the traumas you've lived through, sins you've committed, sins that have been committed against you, and even your ancestors' sins. Think about it. Have you ever committed a sin or gone through a horrible trauma and afterward felt oppressed and overloaded in your soul? That's because what you did or were subjected to slammed down your gates, thus the dunamis power that's in you can't flow into those places to heal you.

Here's an example: When a person watches pornography, vile images enter into his eye gate, his imagination, and his memory. Once these images enter the gate, they often control that person and bring total destruction. Sadly countless Christians are obsessed with porn. Many of them have told me that pornography is one of the hardest addictions to overcome. That's because when this sin slams their gates shut, the dunamis power that's in them can't freely flow into those areas to bring healing and deliverance from that addiction.

What are you letting in your eye gate? Are you watching movies and TV shows that are full of sexual content and immorality? How about your ear gate? Do you let yourself listen to gossip, cursing, vulgarity, or even a bad report? What are you releasing out of your mouth gate? Is it bitterness, offense, or criticism? Have you been letting your imagination meditate on revenge, evil, or perversion of some kind?

You need to be careful what you allow in all your gates because sin and trauma of any kind can shut them down and prevent the power that's in you from moving like a river throughout your entire being.

OPENING THE GATES

Once the gates are shut, how do you open them? By believing in the finished work of Christ and the power of His blood. Jesus already opened the gates for us, and through His blood we can apply His victory on the cross to all our gates so that the living water in us can bring breakthrough. Let's look at how Jesus opened the very first entryway into your being. We will start with the model of the first temple, the tabernacle in the desert. This structure was built in three parts.

- The most holy place is where the ark, which contained the presence of the Lord, was kept.

- The holy place is where the menorah, the incense burner, and the showbread table were placed.

- The outer court contained the brazen altar.

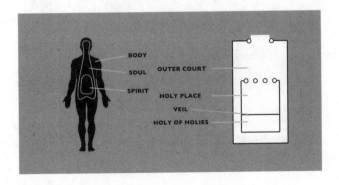

Now look at the image. The three parts of the tabernacle correspond to your three-part being. Your spirit man is the most holy place, where the presence of the Lord lives now. Your soul is the holy place, and your body is the outer court.

What does this have to do with opening gates? Look again at the image. Do you see what was hanging in between the most holy place and the holy place? It was a veil that blocked everyone but the high priest from accessing the ark and entering the presence of God. Yet when Jesus died on the cross and shed His blood, the veil of the temple was torn in two:

> Then, behold, the veil of the temple was torn in two from top to bottom; and the earth quaked, and the rocks were split.
>
> —MATTHEW 27:51

The blood Jesus shed on the cross ripped the veil that was between the most holy place and the holy place. This removed the blockage that was hindering people from coming confidently into the presence of the Lord.

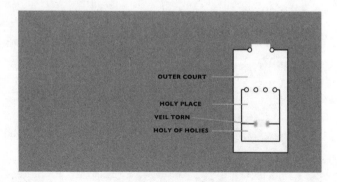

That's why the Bible says that now we can "come boldly to the throne of grace, that we may obtain mercy and find grace to help in time of need" (Heb. 4:16).

The blood removed the veil, which today gives us access to the power and presence of God. Believe it or not, before you were born again, your spiritual temple also had a veil in it. That veil was in between your spirit (the most holy place) and your soul (the holy place). But when you received Christ as Lord, that veil was removed! Look at proof from 2 Corinthians 3:16: "But whenever a person turns [in repentance] to the Lord, the veil is stripped off and taken away" (AMPC).

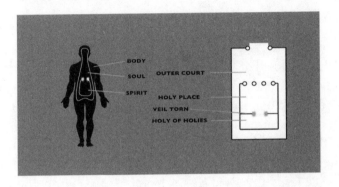

Look at the third image. Once you have repented and received Jesus as your Lord and Savior, His blood rips the veil in you, just as it did the veil in the temple. So what did that accomplish? It enabled the dunamis resurrection power that is in your spirit to escape its confinements and begin to flow like rivers of living water into your soul to transform you from glory to glory into the image and likeness of Christ, as 2 Corinthians 3:18 says:

> But we all, with unveiled face, beholding as in a mirror the glory of the Lord, are being transformed into the same image from glory to glory, just as by the Spirit of the Lord.

Jesus opened the first door in you that was blocking the flow of the rivers of living waters. The reason your soul and the rest of your body can be healed now is because the veil was ripped. In fact, the opening of this first gate in you is the hope and anchor for the healing of your soul. Look at this amazing verse in Hebrews 6:19:

> This hope we have as an anchor for our soul, both sure and steadfast, and which enters the Presence behind the veil.

Do you see that? The hope we have as an anchor of healing for our soul is that Jesus ripped the veil!

The Lord opened the first gate in you with His precious blood. The blood has the power to cleanse every sin or trauma that could ever close your gates. In fact, the blood acts like a key that unlocks those doors so they can be lifted up and the King of glory can come in.

Since Jesus already shed His blood for all the sins you have ever committed at your gates, you can now labor to enter into His rest through your repentance and faith in His finished work. As you repent for any sin that took place at your gates, believe your sins have already been forgiven. Then decree that all your gates are slathered with the blood. After this you can do as Psalm 24 instructs and command your ancient gates to be lifted up so that the King of glory (Jesus and His dunamis power that lives in you) can come in.

MY ANCIENT GATES

Let me tell you the story that helped me understand this biblical truth about ancient gates. I was traveling back from a meeting in Pennsylvania and had a layover in Chicago. I was born there but hadn't set foot in that city since I was a little girl. While I was on the plane, the Lord unexpectedly said, "There's an enemy waiting for you at the gate in Chicago."

As soon as I landed, I was viciously attacked. I could hardly breathe as my throat swelled up. It was so painful that I couldn't swallow or talk, and excruciating waves of pain shot through my whole body. As I walked to the next gate to catch my next plane for the second leg of my flight, I was praying "Dunamis, dunamis, dunamis," in my mind, but it wasn't helping.

All the way home I commanded my soul to become excellent and my body to receive a miracle, yet the assault would not break. I was in so much agony that when my husband picked me up at the airport, I threw my head on his chest and wept. (I am not a crybaby, so that shows how bad it was.)

For two weeks straight I lay on the floor of my living room, worshipping for hours in an attempt to get healed. The surround speakers in my ceiling were so loud I could literally feel the music pulsating through my body. Yet I stayed as sick as ever! One night there was so much heavenly glory and light in the room that my skin turned red and I looked as if I had been sunburned!

However, despite the level of power in my house, I remained as sick as before. "How is that possible?" I asked myself. What in the world was blocking me from receiving my healing with that level of glory present?

Three days afterward I was going to visit a relative when I had to pull over to get gas. I started asking God what was going on with my body, and He said, "Command that ancient gate to be lifted up."

"What does that mean?" I responded.

He simply said, "Psalm 24."

I quickly looked it up on my cell phone, and sure enough, it talked about commanding the ancient gates to be lifted up.

Not knowing any better, I started doing just that. Within sixty seconds the pain and swelling in my throat and the aches in my body completely dissipated.

I came to understand that there were ancient gates inside me that had been shut since birth. When I landed in Chicago, where I was born, my presence triggered my ancient wounds and the demons that were attached to them. The reason I couldn't get healed even though there was massive power in my house was because there was an ancient gate inside me that was closed. It was preventing the dunamis power in my spirit from flowing into that wounded area.

Remember, wounds can be passed down through your bloodline, so you may have *ancient* gates inside you that you received in the womb, and they may be causing all kinds of issues. If so, it's time to open them up.

THE ENEMY AT THE GATE

As I've mentioned before, soul wounds give the enemy a legal right to assault you. One of Satan's goals is to take possession of your gates. Deuteronomy 28:52 confirms this truth:

> They shall besiege you at all your gates until your high and fortified walls, in which you trust, come down throughout all your land; and they shall besiege you at all your gates.

Evil spirits can take control of your gates when there is a wound inside you that gives them the legal right to do so. Once they attach themselves to a wound, they hide behind the closed gate, where they are safe because dunamis power can't get to them.

One time I was having severe problems with my mind, so

I asked God to show me what the source was. In a vision He took me to a house, which I knew represented my intellect. He allowed me to see the situation from the inside out. As I stood in the hallway, I saw an enemy combatant crouching behind the front door, which of course was closed. That's when I knew Satan had taken possession of that gate.

So I simply repented for any way in which I might have used my intellect that was outside the will of God and then decreed that the door was slathered with the blood of Jesus. Then I commanded it to be lifted up. Once the dunamis power flowed into that place, I felt a major shift, and peace filled my mind as the demon fled.

GATE TESTIMONIES

A man who was swollen, greasy, and gray-looking because his liver wasn't functioning properly and bile was backing up into his body came to one of my meetings. It was horrible. That night I was teaching on the subject of ancient gates. He was sitting in the front row, and I walked over and pointed at him and said, "I command those ancient gates inside of you to be lifted up." Instantly I saw a vision of a big, ancient gate lifting up a few feet from the ground and water flowing through it.

When I glanced back down at him, he looked as if he had seen a ghost. When I asked him what happened, he said, "As soon as you said that, I saw a gate. It didn't open like a door on its hinges. It lifted up just like you told it to, and water began flowing through it!"

He had seen the exact same thing I did. He had an ancient gate in him that was closed, but when it lifted up, rivers of living water flowed from his innermost being into that place and healed him. He lost fifteen pounds of bile weight in twenty-four hours. Then he dropped sixteen more over the next two weeks. He was completely healed and was able to go back to work to support his family.

I witnessed another gate miracle at a different meeting. A woman who was attending woke up that morning in her hotel with a familiar situation. She couldn't see out of one eye. Her vision was completely dark except for a ring of light around the edge of the darkness. She had experienced it before in her other eye, so she knew what was going on: her retina was detaching from her eye.

She had to make a decision whether to rush to the doctor or go to the meeting. She chose the latter. That day I was teaching on the ancient gates. When she prayed through the activation with me and commanded her soul gates and eye gate to be lifted up, her retina immediately reattached, and her sight was fully restored!

PRAYER ACTIVATION

Below is a list of body gates and soul gates. Go through every one on both lists and repent to God for any sin you committed at those gates. As you do, believe Jesus has already forgiven you, then receive the power of His finished work on the cross. Remember, God's Word confirms that you have been freely justified by His blood (Rom. 3:24–25). This verse means you are already forgiven, and now it's up to you to believe it and receive it. Decree that the blood of Jesus is on every one of your gates, and command them to be lifted up so the King of glory can come in. You can use the prayer provided or your own words.

Body gates
Eye gate, ear gate, nose gate, mouth gate, senses gate

Soul gates

Subconscious mind, conscious mind, memory, intellect, reasoning, imagination, the will, emotions, passions, and desires

> *I decree that Jesus has already shed His blood for every sin and trauma that closed down my gates. With His blood Jesus tore the veil between my spirit man and my soul. Now dunamis power can get out and flow like rivers of living water from my innermost being through my soul to make it excellent and then into my body to quicken it. I decree that the blood is on every one of my gates, and I command them all to be lifted up now so the King of glory can come in with His dunamis power to heal me and set me free! In Jesus's name, amen.*

Chapter 9

YOUR POWER OVER LEGION

A T ONE POINT in my life I was very sick on and off for almost a year. For long periods of time, sometimes months, I would experience fevers and extreme body pain. My throat would swell with agonizing inflammation that was accompanied by thick, sticky mucus. This unexplainable illness would come in like a flood with seemingly no end. Even the strongest antibiotics had no effect. Then, just as quickly as it began, it would mysteriously vanish, only to return a few months later. This process repeated itself over and over again, leaving me exhausted and completely baffled.

The illness was also accompanied by a severe case of vertigo that left me totally incapacitated. I had experienced the same thing years before. Right after I got out of prison, I started having vertigo. Even the slightest movement of my head would make me feel as if everything around me was spinning. It got so bad that my mom finally convinced me to go to a physician. After being tested, I was diagnosed with lupus, a disease in which the body attacks and destroys itself. Once I got the news, the Lord told me not to return to the doctors but to trust Him.

During that time I had a dream about my father, whom I hadn't seen for twenty years. In the dream I was wandering around a bunch of old tombstones. When I woke up, I heard this verse: "And when he was come out of the ship, immediately there met him out of the tombs a man with an unclean spirit" (Mark 5:2, KJV). It was from the story of the demoniac who was being controlled by the spirit of Legion. I had no idea what God was trying to tell me, but a week later the power of the Lord fell on me, and the vertigo went away and I was healed of lupus.

Yet three years later all the symptoms and more came back with a vengeance, as I described at the beginning of the chapter. In the middle of those assaults I had so much noise and worthless chatter in my mind that I could not hear God's voice at all. I was desperate for a word, knowing that just one would solve the problem I was dealing with.

So day after day I pressed in, hoping His voice would finally pierce through the nonsensical madness in my brain. Then finally in the midst of the noise I heard the Lord say, "Put him under torment." I had a feeling "him" was the spirit that was making me sick. So I rushed to the privacy of my bathroom and started tormenting the devil the best I knew how—by threatening him with everything from stabbing his eyes out with hot pokers to digging out his liver with a spoon to kicking him in the crotch with my steel-toed boots. (God took the girl out of the street, but He didn't take all the street out of the girl.)

Sure enough, my mind got quiet, and I said, "Hurry up, God, and tell me what it is before he comes back!"

Immediately I heard, "Mark 5:7." This verse records the moment when Jesus was face-to-face with the spirit of Legion and that spirit said to Him, "What have You to do with me, Jesus, Son of the Most High God? [What is there in common between us?] I solemnly implore you by God, do not begin to torment me!" (AMPC).

This verse showed me two things: it was Legion attacking

me again because I had something in my soul that was in common with him, and he hated to be tormented, which is why he shut up when I put the heat on. His noisy voice returned soon afterward, but it was too late for him. I had already started to get a revelation that would eventually lead me to totally kick his butt.

DOING BATTLE WITH LEGION

Winning the battle against Legion is so important to soul healing that I want to share the entire story of the demoniac with you from the classic edition of the Amplified Bible.

> They came to the other side of the sea to the region of the Gerasenes. And as soon as He got out of the boat, there met Him out of the tombs a man [under the power] of an unclean spirit.
>
> This man continually lived among the tombs, and no one could subdue him any more, even with a chain; for he had been bound often with shackles for the feet and handcuffs, but the handcuffs of [light] chains he wrenched apart, and the shackles he rubbed and ground together and broke in pieces; and no one had strength enough to restrain or tame him.
>
> Night and day among the tombs and on the mountains he was always shrieking and screaming and beating and bruising and cutting himself with stones. And when from a distance he saw Jesus, he ran and fell on his knees before Him in homage, and crying out with a loud voice, he said, What have You to do with me, Jesus, Son of the Most High God? [What is there in common between us?] I solemnly implore you by God, do not begin to torment me! For Jesus was commanding, Come out of the man, you unclean spirit!

And He asked him, What is your name? He replied, My name is Legion, for we are many. And he kept begging Him urgently not to send them [himself and the other demons] away out of that region.

Now a great herd of hogs was grazing there on the hillside. And the demons begged Him, saying, Send us to the hogs, that we may go into them! So He gave them permission. And the unclean spirits came out [of the man] and entered into the hogs; and the herd, numbering about 2,000, rushed headlong down the steep slope into the sea and were drowned in the sea.

The hog feeders ran away, and told [it] in the town and in the country. And [the people] came to see what it was that had taken place. And they came to Jesus and looked intently and searchingly at the man who had been a demoniac, sitting there, clothed and in his right mind, [the same man] who had had the legion [of demons]; and they were seized with alarm and struck with fear.

And those who had seen it related in full what had happened to the man possessed by demons and to the hogs. And they began to beg [Jesus] to leave their neighborhood. And when He had stepped into the boat, the man who had been controlled by the unclean spirits kept begging Him that he might be with Him. But Jesus refused to permit him, but said to him, Go home to your own [family and relatives and friends] and bring back word to them of how much the Lord has done for you, and [how He has] had sympathy for you and mercy on you.

And he departed and began to publicly proclaim in Decapolis [the region of the ten cities] how much Jesus had done for him, and all the people were astonished and marveled.

—MARK 5:1–20

Notice that when the demoniac was delivered, he sat at Jesus's feet clothed and in his right mind (v. 15). The phrase "right mind" is the Greek word *sōphroneō*, which means "to be of sound mind."[1] Clearly he was not in his right mind when he was being tormented by this spirit. That's because Legion—which is actually a group of many spirits—causes everything from depression and anxiety to bipolar disease. He has the ability to negatively affect the functions of the mind and control the way you feel and the actions you take.

Look what Legion made the demoniac do to himself: he lived naked among the tombs; he beat, bruised, and cut himself; he was always shrieking and screaming and grinding up the shackles that were meant to bind him (vv. 3–5). He was also so violent that no one could restrain or tame him (v. 3). The demoniac was totally out of control because he was being mentally and physically controlled and tormented by Legion. Yet after a short encounter with Jesus he was delivered and sat there clothed and in his right mind (v. 15).

If you are suffering from any sort of mental disorder, it may be Legion at work, as it was for a man at one of the meetings where I was a guest. For many years the man had been tormented by an extreme bipolar disorder. His mind was never quiet, and he was in constant anguish. If he wasn't depressed, he was extremely manic. His behavior had put a huge strain on all his relationships. During a session another speaker asked me to help pray for people in the audience. I started walking through the crowd and touching them. When I got to him, the Lord specifically had me put both my hands on his head. When I did, Legion fled, and the man was instantly healed. Years later I met him again, and he told me that his whole life dramatically changed at that moment.

LEGION ATTACKS YOUR MIND

Legion is like a tweeker on meth. He is constantly chattering, filling our minds with endless noise. Think about it: out of every demon mentioned in the whole Bible, he said the most.

"Jesus, what is there in common between us?" (See Mark 5:7.)

"Please don't torment me." (See Mark 5:7.)

"Don't send us out of the region." (See Mark 5:10.)

"Send us into the pigs." (See Mark 5:12.)

Legion is constantly talking. Many times he will put negative thoughts and accusations into your mind to tear you down and devalue you. Since he talks in the first person, you think it's your own thoughts. "I messed up again." "I'm worthless." "I am not attractive." "I have no skills or gifts." "Nobody loves me."

The enemy wants to make you feel bad about yourself. His goal is to get you to come into agreement with what he is telling you so you won't believe what the Bible says about you. The truth according to the Scriptures is that you are a beloved son or daughter of the Most High, you are the righteousness of God in Christ, and you have dunamis power in you that will enable you to do all things through Him who strengthens you (Phil. 4:13). Legion uses his words to try to conform you into his image instead of the image of Jesus Christ. If he can get you to embrace what he is saying, it will be only so long before you become what you believe.

He also puts nonsensical chatter in your mind so you can't hear the voice of God. Legion wants to block you from getting the revelation that will free you from Satan's control. One word from God can break through every resistance, heal every disease, and position you to totally defeat the enemy. Legion tries to make your mind so noisy that you can't hear the download you need to get the victory. I had to put Legion under torment just to get him to quiet down for a minute so I could hear God tell me it was him!

LEGION BRINGS PHYSICAL ILLNESS

The Bible says that when the demoniac was delivered of Legion, he sat there "clothed and in his right mind" (Mark 5:15, AMPC). In the etymology of the phrase *right mind* (*sōphroneō*) is the Greek word *sōzō,* which means, "to save…one suffering from disease, to make well, heal, restore to health."[2] Legion doesn't attack just your mind; he goes after your body as well. A Roman legion was made up of six thousand soldiers. The spirit of Legion has tons of troops that cause viruses, bacterial diseases, and physical problems of all kinds. He was the spirit responsible for my lupus as well as the vertigo and extreme flu-like symptoms I was experiencing. My entire life I suffered from the flu. I would get it three times a year even when it wasn't flu season. I also had chronic bladder and yeast infections. Now that I have been healed and delivered from this spirit, I don't suffer from any of those disorders anymore!

One time I was so sick with a combination of the flu and yeast and bladder infections that I asked God to show me what was causing it. Immediately He opened my eyes, and I saw a green demon that looked almost exactly like Slimer from the movie *Ghostbusters.* The Lord revealed that it was one of the many soldiers in Legion's numbers. It was breathing a green cloud of bacteria on me that was making me sick.

Have you ever thought about how easily the flu spreads? Legion carries it with him as he jumps from one person to the next, spreading the virus as he goes. He is a mover and a shaker in a bad way. Look at how mobile he was when Jesus confronted him. He went from the demoniac to the pigs and then from the pigs to the water (Mark 5:12–13). He is able to travel from one being and location to the next, releasing disease as he goes.

Before I was totally healed of Legion, I went to a meeting where everybody had the flu, and I was also very sick. I knew it was Legion, but I couldn't stop him. At that time I was not totally healed of everything I had in common with him. Yet I wanted to help those people because they were so miserable. I decided to line everyone up and pray for them anyway. It didn't go well. No one was healed; instead, they were all worse than ever.

After we took a lunch break, two ladies came running up to me with a look of fear on their faces. They said, "While you were praying over everybody, we were recording you. Then at lunch we played it back, and we could hear pigs in the background grunting!" One of the women added that her husband walked into the room while they were listening and said, "What's that? Sounds like a bunch of pigs!" I had not said a word to anyone that it was Legion we were dealing with.

I used to be afraid of Legion because he seemed so powerful and invincible. However, once the Lord showed me what was allowing him to assault my life, I came to see him as a little cockroach being crushed under my foot.

So what gives Legion the legal right to batter believers? Not surprisingly, the wounded soul.

Dwelling Among the Tombs

Three times in Mark 5 we see a reference to the fact that the demoniac dwelled among the tombs:

> And when he was come out of the ship, immediately
> there met him *out of the tombs* a man with an unclean
> spirit, who had his dwelling *among the tombs*; and no
> man could bind him…and always, night and day, he
> was in the mountains, and *in the tombs*.
>   —MARK 5:2–3, 5, KJV, EMPHASIS ADDED

When the Bible says something three times, you need to pay special attention to it! What does the word *tombs* refer to? The Greek word used in the Scriptures is *mnēmeion*, which means "any visible object for preserving or recalling the memory of any person or thing."[3] Tombs are unhealed areas in your inner man that cause you to continually hold on to and recall the memory of a painful relationship or event. They are the reminders of the horrible things that happened in your past that should be long dead and buried but instead are alive in your mind and are totally controlling you. You will know if you have a tomb in your soul because you will find yourself constantly going to the "graveyard" to sit in front of that tombstone to grieve, mourn, and lament.

The demoniac was dwelling among the tombs. He was living in the pain of his past. The word "dwell" in the Scriptures is the Greek word *katoikeō*, which means "divine powers, influences…[that] dwell in his [a person's] soul, to pervade, prompt, govern it."[4]

Legion was able to influence, prompt, and govern the demoniac because his soul was wounded. He was dwelling on the pain and agony of his past traumas and hurtful situations, which gave Legion the legal right to devastate his life.

Are you still living in your past? Is your mind constantly dwelling on painful things that happened to you? Are you unable to get over an offense, a rejection, a divorce, or the memory of a lost loved one? If so, then you are dwelling among the tombs and giving Legion the right to assault you.

What is the condition of your physical health? Do you have pain or disease of any kind? Do you get bacterial infections or viruses a lot? How about sinus problems or allergies? Maybe you have problems with bladder or yeast infections? Do you have constant water-weight issues or edema? Are you suffering from a mental disorder? Do you have chatter in your brain? Even worse, are you doing what the demoniac did, screaming, beating, and bruising yourself? All these manifestations are evidence of Legion's influence.

Legion drove the demoniac to cut himself. Do you know why teens today are doing the same? It's because they are dwelling among the tombs. Many teens are wounded because their parents got divorced, they are being bullied by school-mates, or they have a horrible self-image, particularly related to their bodies. Today's teens want to look like the stars they admire, and if they don't, the peer pressure becomes too much to bear. They are wounded in their inner man, and their wounds enable Legion to drive them to mutilate themselves.

HAVE NOTHING IN COMMON WITH THE ENEMY

When we are dwelling among the tombs, we have something in our souls that is "in common" with the enemy. This gives him the right to attack us. Jesus made it clear that this was *not* true of Him:

> I will not talk with you much more, for the prince (evil genius, ruler) of the world is coming. And he has no claim on Me. [He has nothing in common with Me;

there is nothing in Me that belongs to him, and he has no power over Me.]

—JOHN 14:30, AMPC

Here Jesus gives us the key to supernatural deliverance: have nothing in your soul that is in common with Satan, and he will have no power over you. Jesus had nothing in Him that was in common with Legion, so that spirit had no power over Him. Mark 5:6–7 describes what happened when Jesus and Legion came face-to-face:

And when from a distance he saw Jesus, he ran and fell on his knees before Him in homage, and crying out with a loud voice, he said, What have You to do with me, Jesus, Son of the Most High God? [What is there in common between us?] I solemnly implore you by God, do not begin to torment me!

—MARK 5:6–7, AMPC

Legion recognized the truth of Jesus's statement in John 14. He knew that our Lord had nothing in Him that was in common with Satan. Thus Legion could not torment Jesus—but Jesus could torment him!

Do you want a spirit as big as Legion to beg you not to torment him? He will when you get your soul healed. Then you will have nothing in common with him, so he will have no power over you.

When people get delivered from the spirit of Legion, unusual signs accompany their healing. Water comes running out of their eyes, ears, nose, and other parts of their bodies. Later I will explain why. But for now let me share some testimonies.

One woman experienced a major miracle in my meeting when she was delivered of Legion. She had suffered loss and had dealt with a lot of stress and anxiety from living through two major storms. She thought she had dealt with the grief and been healed.

However, she realized that she was still carrying the memories of those storms. A few days before the conference she had come down with shingles and had sores and bruises all over her body. In the activation we were working on healing the tombs in our pasts. When she prayed, water came out of her eyes, and she discovered she had received a miracle.

She went into the bathroom to check for shingles and found that there were no marks or scars left. In fact, it was as if she had never had it in the first place!

Another woman had been having headaches every day for sixteen years and always felt a throbbing in her right ear that was so loud she could hear it. She'd wake up feeling OK, but by the evening she'd have a headache and would have to lie down or at least close her eyes for thirty minutes just to keep going. When she came to the meeting, it was evening, and as usual she had a headache and could hear the pulsating in her ear. But after we prayed the activations, she felt water start to drain down her neck near her ear as well as down her throat. It was so much water that she had to keep swallowing. When the water stopped draining, both the noise in her ear and her headache were gone! She had been delivered of Legion!

A woman named Jolene had suffered from severe chronic allergies and asthma for most of her life. She regularly experienced severe asthmatic coughing spells and was often winded just by having a normal conversation. She said she felt as if she always had an elephant sitting on her chest. The asthma had been exceptionally bad the week she came to my meeting. In fact, she wasn't sure she was going to make it.

At one point I asked the Lord to "heal everyone's tombs." Jolene kept repeating, "I forgive them" over and over concerning all the people who had hurt her. All of a sudden she felt a great amount of mucus and water drain from her head and sinus area into her throat. When she breathed in, there was no pain or congestion, and she could breathe easily through her nose. The elephant was gone! In addition, she said she didn't feel emotionally hurt anymore! Previously when she thought of those who had wounded her, she would feel pain, but the feelings of anger, pain, and resentment had vanished. She had been healed from her tombs and delivered of Legion!

LEGION IS A REGIONAL DEMON

Some demons are over entire regions of land. They have been assigned to guard those areas and afflict the people who live there. Legion is one of them. Look again at what he said to Jesus: "And he kept begging Him urgently not to send them [himself and the other demons] away out of that region" (Mark 5:10, AMPC).

Legion was assigned to guard the region of the Gerasenes, which is east of Galilee, and he didn't want to be removed. That's why he begged Jesus not to send him out of the region.

Have you ever gone on a missionary trip and gotten sick? When believers travel to new places to minister, they are often met by regional spirits that try to stop them. This is what happened to Jesus the day He encountered Legion:

> They came to the other side of the sea to the region of the Gerasenes. And as soon as He got out of the boat, there met Him out of the tombs a man [under the power] of an unclean spirit.
>
> —MARK 5:1–2, AMPC

Jesus was going to minister in the region of the Gerasenes, and as soon as He stepped out of the boat, He was met by Legion, the regional demon assigned to the area. Legion immediately ran up to Jesus because that's what regional spirits do. As soon as a believer enters their territory, they immediately examine him to see if there is anything in his soul that can be used to assault him. That's why the first thing Legion said to Jesus was, "What is there in common between us?...Do not begin to torment me" (v. 7). When he took a good look at Christ, he found no soul wound he could use to stop the Lord from ministering in that region of land.

When I first began to travel in ministry, I would encounter Legion every time I went to a new region. As soon as I would step out of a boat or an airplane or a car, this spirit would meet me. His goal was to find something in my soul he could use to make me physically ill so he could stop me. Once when I went to Virginia, I got the flu, a swollen throat, vertigo, and bladder and yeast infections, all within one hour of landing in the state!

Another minister I met had a similar experience, but she received a miracle during one of my meetings. As she stood in line to testify, her eyes and nose started to water. When she reached me on stage, she reported that she had suffered from a recurring bladder infection for many years. She said that it always seemed to flare up when she set foot in a different region. Her testimony confirmed that Legion had been assaulting her whenever she ministered in a new area of land, but she was healed that day, so he no longer had any hold on her.

I have heard some horror stories about missionaries who go overseas and get attacked so severely they end up dying. One man I knew was in perfect health when he went to India. Within weeks of his return, he suddenly developed ALS. Eventually the disease took his life after causing him a great deal of suffering.

If you're going to try to take a region in a different

neighborhood, state, or country, get some soul healing before you go. Then you'll have nothing in you that is in common with the regional demons assigned to guard those places.

One way to determine whether you're really healed is to get together with your family for a holiday or family event. Many people get sick or mentally and emotionally afflicted when they attend a family gathering or reunion. If this happens to you, it's a sign you're dwelling among the tombs of the past history in your family and giving Legion cause to attack you.

REGIONS OF WOUNDED PEOPLE

Do you know how regional demons get their legal right to be over entire regions of land? The people in those places are dwelling among the tombs. In the region of the Gerasenes the demoniac wasn't the only person who was wounded; the rest of the people in that area were as well. When Jesus sent Legion into the pigs and they drowned themselves, the pig keepers ran off and told people in the city and the country what had happened. So the people came to see for themselves, and they found the demoniac, who had been out of his mind, acting normal (Mark 5:13–15). Then they became afraid and "began to plead with Him [Jesus] to *depart from their region*" (v. 17, emphasis added). They asked Jesus to leave their region. Their words were almost exactly like those Legion used when he begged Jesus not to send him away from the region. What this means is that Legion was speaking to Jesus both times— first through the demoniac and then through the rest of the people in that area. Legion wasn't controlling just the man at the tombs; he was also controlling all the people who lived in that province!

The condition of people's souls in a territory of land gives regional spirits such as Legion the right to control that area.

The world is full of individuals who are hurting, offended, and traumatized and who are dwelling among the tombs, and it's their wounded souls that allow Legion and other spirits to be in control of their lives and the areas of land in which they reside.

No matter where you live or travel to, it's important for you to be healed in your soul so you can walk into any region without experiencing demonic harassment, bring authority and healing to the people there, and kick Legion out.

RECEIVING A MANTLE OF POWER

When you're healed of your past and the tombs you're dwelling among, then you will receive a mantle of power that will enable you to usher in healing, deliverance, and revival wherever you go. Don't forget what happened to the demoniac when he was delivered of Legion: he sat there "clothed and in his right mind" (Mark 5:15, AMPC). The word "clothed" in this verse is the Greek word *himation*, which means "mantle."[5] In the Bible a mantle is a symbol of power and authority. Elijah was a miracle worker who wore a mantle. Once he was taken to heaven, his mantle was passed on to his protégé Elisha, who then performed twice as many miracles as his predecessor.

When you're healed of your tombs and have dominion over Legion, you will receive a mantle of power that will usher in regional revival. Mark 5:20 says that after the demoniac was delivered, he went on to preach the good news of Christ in the ten cities of the region of the Decapolis (AMPC). He became a powerful evangelist and a regional revivalist.

Before I was healed of all the painful memories of my past, I had no power over Legion. In fact, I feared him. He ran over me like a steamroller with sickness and affliction everywhere I went. But today I can walk into a meeting and corporately lead everyone in the room into mass deliverance without laying a hand on a single person. Now I am like the demoniac after he was delivered, clothed and in my right mind, possessing a mantle of power for regional revival!

PRAYER ACTIVATION

Following is the prayer I use in my meetings to get people healed of tombs and then delivered of Legion. I suggest you pray it for yourself right now.

Put your hand on your belly as you make the following declarations. Repeat them as often as you need to until you experience a genuine breakthrough.

I am the righteousness of God in Christ! My sins have been imputed onto Christ. They are not on me anymore.

All the handwritten requirements the enemy uses against me have already been nailed to the cross, and I am full of dunamis power.

I have been given a tankful of dunamis power that never runs out. It makes me excellent of soul.

I release dunamis power from my spirit into these tombs now. It is flowing there, and it is wiping them out and cleansing them. I am excellent of soul.

I'm putting dunamis power to work. It is strengthening and reinforcing my inner man.

I am putting dunamis power to work in healing all my memories, emptying all my tombs, and freeing me from all the pain of my past.

Every tomb in which I have been dwelling is now obliterated. I am healed!

I am now in position to have all the superabundance that Jesus has for me!

I have nothing in me that is in common with Satan or Legion, so they must go now!

I am clothed with a mantle of power to bring in regional revival wherever I go! I decree soul healing for the wounded people in every region I minister in. In Jesus's name, amen and amen.

Chapter 10

SOUL REMEDY FOR EATING DISORDERS

I HAD MAJOR FOOD issues from the time I was young. I always ate too much but was never satisfied. I would also wolf down my food like a starving animal, acting as if I were afraid someone was going to take it from me.

On my tenth birthday my mom made me a meal consisting of a huge porterhouse steak that took up an entire platter with an equal-size baked potato to match. For dessert I had a half gallon of vanilla ice cream, still in the carton, surrounded by a half dozen huge vanilla-glazed donuts. I ate every bite at superhigh speed.

Sometimes on special occasions my parents would drive us an hour away to a fancy steakhouse. I always ordered the biggest portion of meat on the menu, cut off a huge piece, stuffed it in my mouth, chewed twice, and then swallowed. I repeated this process at record speed over and over, despite the protests of my mother, who told me I would choke to death one day if I kept it up. Then she would follow that statement with, "I hope you're wearing clean underwear when the ambulance comes."

As a teen I went to a local ice cream parlor. They had a dish called the "pig trough," which consisted of six scoops of ice cream, two bananas, toppings, whipped cream, and big cherries with nuts all around. If you ate one by yourself, the waitresses came out and sang, "You're a pig. You're a pig. You're a really big pig." To their amazement—and disgust—I once ate three in a row by myself.

Even when I was a meth addict on the streets, I ate like a beast. Speed normally takes away your appetite, so most addicts get very thin while abusing it. Not me! I would do a spoonful and then say, "Hey, man, let's go to 7-Eleven and get a few chili cheese dogs."

When I was in prison, I practically starved to death. The food had zero nutritional value and was just plain gross. A few times we even discovered maggots in our chow. That's not surprising since the shipments of food that came into the kitchen had "For Inmate Consumption Only" stamped on the boxes.

After I was released, I went crazy buying food. The grocery stores were filled with new items that had been developed while I was inside, and I wanted to try them all. Walking through the aisles felt like being in Disneyland on crack. Plus, all the fast-food restaurants had something new called "supersizing." Of course that led me to order combo meals in the largest size available.

Even after the ministry was established, I battled with food addiction. Once I was in a meeting that didn't end until midnight. Afterward we got something to eat (as always), and I ordered a massive amount of food. While we waited, some people from the meeting came into the restaurant. They watched as the waitress served our food, which filled the entire table. Wasting no time, I grabbed half of a sandwich and shoved the whole thing in my mouth. The people across the way dropped their jaws in shock. I'm sure it blew their positive image of me right out of the water.

It was a good thing I had a high metabolism and would expend huge amounts of energy while preaching because the most I gained was about twenty-five pounds, which to many people is not a lot, but on my small frame it was. However, I was still completely tormented by the bizarre hold food had on me. I always wanted more and couldn't stop thinking about it.

FOOD ADDICTIONS ARE
MEANT TO DESTROY US

I know my story isn't unique. Millions of people are struggling with food issues. They are addicted to stuff that is really bad for them, including sugar, junk food, and fast food. They are controlled by their cravings for food and have tried to lose weight with no success.

Sadly food addictions can lead to serious illnesses and even death. Obesity can increase a person's risk of heart disease, high blood pressure, diabetes, high cholesterol, cancer, sleep apnea, back pain, and much, much more.[1]

News flash: this is just what Satan wants!

His sole mission is to steal, kill, and destroy (John 10:10), and one of the ways he carries this out is by causing us to be controlled by food. After all, he used a simple piece of fruit to cause the fall of the entire human race! The Bible says that he tempted Eve to eat the fruit from a tree in the garden that God had told her and Adam was off-limits:

> And when the woman saw that the tree was good for food, and that it was pleasant to the eyes, and a tree to be desired to make one wise, she took of the fruit thereof, and did eat, and gave also unto her husband with her; and he did eat.
>
> —GENESIS 3:6, KJV

The strategy Satan used with Eve was so successful that he still uses food today to control, shame, and destroy us. In fact, he has employed it throughout the ages. In ancient times the practice of idolatry—the worship of false gods—was very common. When pagans held ceremonies to celebrate these false gods, or idols, they would dedicate food to them. This was not an innocent exercise since the Bible says the idols they worshipped were really demon spirits. During these ceremonies people would eat the food that was dedicated to these demons because it was a way for them to become one with those evil spirits. The apostle Paul warned the people of the Corinthians church about this practice:

> I am suggesting that what the pagans sacrifice they offer [in effect] to demons (to evil spiritual powers) and not to God [at all]. I do not want you to fellowship and be partners with diabolical spirits [by eating at their feasts].
> —1 Corinthians 10:20, ampc

Believers today are not likely to find themselves eating food that was sacrificed to idols, but we can still engage in the sin of gluttony—and then essentially partner with demons—by "feasting," or overeating. When we do, we open the door to a demonic attack.

I can't tell you how many times I have allowed myself to feast excessively and then had a sudden flare-up of pain in my body. When you chronically overindulge, you are doing what Paul warned against, fellowshipping and being partners with diabolical spirits "by eating at their feasts" (1 Cor. 10:20, ampc). If you have a habit of overeating, I suggest that you take communion, and as you do, declare that you are fellowshipping not with demons but with the body and blood of Jesus (1 Cor. 10:16). Then the demonic assault on your body will break.

I have also battled against spirits that put thoughts in my mind to eat more. Not every thought you have is your own. The enemy wants to drive you to eat so he will have a legal right to assault you and even make you sick.

One weekend several months after I had been in the car accident I described in a previous chapter, I couldn't stop eating. I would grab something from the cupboard, finish it off, and then find myself in front of the refrigerator ten minutes later. At first I thought I was just hungry because my body was healing from the accident, but then God let me see what was really going on.

As I was heading to the refrigerator again, the Lord opened my eyes to see a spirit standing to my side with a Green Beret hat on, eating a chocolate-covered éclair. He was glaring at me and saying under his breath, "Yeah, eat more." I realized then that he was the voice in my head telling me to eat and eat and eat.

In the natural realm the Green Berets are a Special Forces unit, highly skilled and trained. Satan has his own special units, including demons whose goal is to drive you to consume more food than you need so they can gain a legal right to devastate or even take your life.

THE CAUSE OF EATING DISORDERS

Why does food have such a hold on us? Because our souls are so wounded that we seek to ease the pain in any way we can. So many times we use food to make us feel better or to forget what is bothering us instead of employing God's remedies for healing.

The word "appetite" (*nephesh* in Hebrew) means "the soul, the inner being of man."[2] This indicates that it is our wounded souls that drive our appetites.

Unhealthy cravings and desires are rooted in unhealed emotions and thoughts in our inner man. Think about it: when you're angry or depressed, what do you feel like doing? I used to eat a whole bag of seasoned corn chips with two cans of bean dip to ease the pain in my soul.

Our souls are hungry—starving for comfort, peace, fellowship, love, fulfillment, happiness, and joy. The problem is that in an attempt to fill our mental and emotional needs, we reach for food because eating brings a temporary feeling of satisfaction. Sometimes food and other addictions are the only way we know to ease the pain we feel inside ourselves. However, the momentary comfort eating provides always turns into shame and condemnation. We need to be healed of what ails us so that trauma, bitterness, and generational iniquities will no longer control what and how we eat.

Trauma Drives You to Eat

The soul wounds you receive from experiencing a painful event can compel you to eat. Let me give you an example.

People who have been physically or sexually abused can suffer with major food disorders, such as anorexia, bulimia, or bingeing.[3] The women I did time with in prison are a painful example. A large majority of them had been sexually exploited, and they dealt with their pain through some form of food addiction or related disorder. I had friends inside who would binge and then throw up their food a couple of times a day! What they didn't realize was that their struggle stemmed from the wounds they received during the trauma of their exploitation.

I too was abused as a child. The molestation was so violent I had to have surgery to repair the damage. I don't remember most of it. I do remember, however, that whenever the person who violated me would enter the room, I would run and hide to try to avoid being assaulted again.

The reason people can't always recall molestation or abuse

is that the human subconscious has a safety valve that acti-vates during the assault to protect the soul. Your subcon-scious stores the memory but causes your conscious mind to forget it as a way to enable you to survive the horrible event. The problem is that those memories are still deep in the soul, secretly sabotaging your life. I believe the wounds from the sexual abuse I experienced contributed to my severe bingeing and food addiction. Fortunately I didn't resort to purging. My theory was, "Why waste good food?" But the abuse I suffered, along with food idolatry and bitterness of soul, drove my food and drug habits.

BITTERNESS MAKES YOU FAT

One of the things that drives people to eat and gain weight is bitterness of soul. I experienced this truth in my own life when I began my traveling ministry.

The first four years of tours were brutal. I was out for four days almost every week. During that time I would preach four sessions, take offerings, and pray for countless people. Often I would get only a few hours of sleep because of plane schedules. By the time I got home, I was so exhausted I would pass out cold. After I unpacked, washed my clothes, and then packed again, I would repeat the process. I did this over and over for years.

After a while I got completely burned out and then became totally bitter. There always seemed to be some debacle that happened on each trip. I couldn't go through security at TSA without an incident. Even though I would take off every bit of metal, I always seemed to set off the alarm. Then a TSA officer would pull me to the side and say, "Miss, you need to put your arms up and spread your legs apart so we can pat you down." After doing time in a federal prison, I didn't like hearing "pat you down"! At those moments I could feel the rage rise up in my soul, and it was everything I could do not to rip the security officer's hair off.

The plane trip didn't help either. Flying used to be somewhat glamorous, but today it's more like a cattle call. Everybody is pushing and shoving and mad about everything. You can't even put your seat back without someone screaming at you.

Once you're bitter, you are a magnet for trouble. At the hotel we had something happen on the last night of every single meeting. We called it "the curse of the key." Hotels now give you magnetic key cards rather than metal keys, and it never failed that at the end of two days of preaching my heart out, the key card would stop working. It was midnight by the time I returned to my room, and as always I was exhausted. It didn't help that I still had to pack and would get only a few hours of sleep before I had to leave for the airport. When it happened, I would stand in the hallway, silently screaming at the piece of plastic in my hand. I felt like a mad bull wanting to charge down to the hotel desk and gore the clerk with my horns. By the end of the trip I would be so bitter that I would totally flip out.

Then I started noticing that every time I went away, I gained six or seven pounds. I didn't understand it because I fasted most of the time I was on tour so I could be "holy" for the meetings. (Yet I was as mad as a hornet while I was doing it!) When I came home, I would get on the treadmill and work out hard so I could fit into my clothes before I went on another trip. Then I was back on a plane to do it all over again.

Each time I went away, it was as if I had pulled some invisible rip cord and a life raft had inflated around my midsection. One weekend I came home and had the following week off. I tried to relax, but I was bothered. All I could think about was, why is this happening to me? So I started praying for myself.

I put my hands on my belly and furiously prayed out loud in tongues for three hours, hoping to get an answer and even lose the weight. I was praying so loud that my husband had to keep turning the TV up. He finally looked at me and said, "Can you lose weight somewhere else?"

Just as I was going to give up out of pure exhaustion, my belly suddenly dropped down under my hands. I was shocked. I had instantly lost six pounds!

When I asked God how it happened, He gave me a scripture in Numbers 5. It described a practice used in ancient times to determine whether a married woman had committed adultery. Her husband would bring her to the priest if he suspected she had been unfaithful. To test her, the priest would take a jar full of holy water and put some dust in it from the floor of the tabernacle (vv. 15, 17). He called this concoction "the bitter water that brings a curse" (v. 24). Then he would set it before the woman to drink. If she had not sinned, the bitter water would have no effect on her. However, if she had, *her belly would swell* and her thigh would rot (v. 27).

When I first read the story, I was shocked. But I understood how it applied. We can essentially commit adultery against our heavenly bridegroom by becoming bitter—by choosing sin over our relationship with Him. When we do, our bellies will literally swell and cause us to gain weight.

Many people in my meetings have had the same kind of experience I did when I lost weight supernaturally. They describe it as a "dropping" of their stomachs under their hands, and it happens when they get healed of bitterness.

One woman who had a hugely distended stomach had been experiencing pain because of it. She said it started in her abdomen and then extended right up to her breastbone. In the meeting, I taught on bitterness and then released a word of knowledge, saying, "Distended stomach, go!" Instantly her stomach shrank, and the distension disappeared.

Another time when I was teaching on bitterness, a man came up to testify of something similar that had happened to him. He said the huge bulge in his stomach just suddenly "disappeared" as we were praying. He thought he had lost at least five or ten pounds.

GENERATIONAL FOOD ISSUES

You may be thinking that you can never lose weight because you inherited your body shape and size from your family. But the Bible says you will prosper and be in health even as your soul prospers (3 John 2). This means that when your soul is healed, your physical body will follow suit and even be able to change shape.

Let's look at a biblical account of someone who had major food issues that were passed down to him from an ancestor. The story is about Isaac's son Esau, who gave up his inheritance for food. The Bible indicates that Esau's obsession with food came from his soul and that it was inherited from his father.

Genesis 25:27 describes Esau as "a cunning and skilled hunter, a man of the outdoors" (AMPC). The word "hunter" here is *tsayid* in Hebrew, which means "hunting, game, provision, food."[4] Esau spent his days hunting for food. Clearly he lived in a time when it was necessary to farm and hunt for survival, but Esau seemed to be more food-driven than was warranted. I believe it was his soul that was driving him to constantly seek out something to eat.

Why else would a man forfeit his inheritance for a serving of lentil stew? Genesis 25 describes how readily Esau relinquished his blessing to his twin brother, Jacob, in exchange for food:

Jacob was boiling pottage (lentil stew) one day, when Esau came from the field and was faint [with hunger]. And Esau said to Jacob, I beg of you, let me have some of that red lentil stew to eat, for I am faint and famished!...Jacob answered, Then sell me today your birthright (the rights of a firstborn). Esau said, See here, I am at the point of death; what good can this birthright do me? Jacob said, Swear to me today [that you are selling it to me]; and he swore to [Jacob] and sold him his birthright. Then Jacob gave Esau bread and stew of lentils, and he ate and drank and rose up and went his way. Thus Esau scorned his birthright as beneath his notice.

—GENESIS 25:29–34, AMPC

Twice this passage describes Esau as faint (Hebrew 'ayeph) with hunger. The word *faint* means "to languish" in your soul.[5] *Languish* means "to be or become feeble, weak."[6] So this description indicates that Esau was weak in his soul. When he demanded that Jacob give him some lentil stew, he wasn't physically dying from a lack of food. But his soul was so wounded that he desperately needed the comfort it would bring, even if it meant giving up the vast wealth that would one day be his.

Where did he get his soul wounds? I believe he was born with them because they were passed down from his father. Scripture shows that Isaac too had major soul issues connected to food. The Bible says Isaac loved Esau more than he loved Esau's twin, Jacob. Why? Because "he [Isaac] ate of Esau's game" (Gen. 25:28, AMPC). In other words, Isaac loved Esau more than his brother because Esau brought home the groceries! Isaac's choosing Esau over his brother was in direct opposition to God's will because God had said He loved Jacob and hated Esau (Mal. 1:2–3; Rom. 9:13). But Isaac's soul was so controlled by food that he planned to give the firstborn blessing to the wrong son.

Do you remember the story? Isaac was getting old and about to pass on. Before he died, he told Esau to hunt for his favorite wild game so he could eat before giving Esau his blessing as the firstborn son (Gen. 27:3–4). The problem was that God never intended for Esau to have it, even though he was born first. It was always God's will for Jacob to receive it instead.

When the boys were still in their mother's womb, Rebekah could feel them struggling with each other. The Lord explained to her: "[The founders of] two nations are in your womb, and the separation of two peoples has begun in your body; the one people shall be stronger than the other, and the elder shall serve the younger" (Gen. 25:23, AMPC).

Esau came out first, so he was the elder. Yet God had said the elder would serve the younger. It was God's will that Jacob, not Esau, receive the firstborn blessing. Even though Isaac knew this, he still attempted to give it to Esau. But Rebekah conspired to deceive Isaac into giving Jacob the blessing. Knowing that Isaac could no longer see, she had Jacob put on Esau's clothing so he would smell like his brother. Then she attached goatskins to Jacobs's arms so he would feel hairy like Esau and sent Jacob in to fool Isaac into blessing him instead (Gen. 27:3–30).

The firstborn blessing was serious business to God because Jesus Christ was to come out of the line of Jacob, not out of the line of Esau. But Isaac's obsession with food drove him to try to put the blessing on the bloodline that didn't lead to Christ.

Isaac even made the execution of the blessing all about food. He told Esau: "Now therefore take, I pray thee, thy weapons, thy quiver and thy bow, and go out to the field, and take me some venison; and make me savoury meat, such as I love, and bring it to me, that I may eat; that my soul may bless thee before I die" (Gen. 27:3–4, KJV). Isaac's promise of blessing had a condition—that Esau would go hunt some venison and make it into savory meat for Isaac to eat so that his *soul* could then bless his son.

It is clear that the wounds in Isaacs's soul were passed down to Esau because Esau was equally controlled by food and ended up doing something just as drastic as his father did. He gave up his birthright—massive wealth, power, and authority—for a meal.

Then what was in Esau's soul was passed down to his descendants, the Edomites. The main idol the Edomites worshipped was the goat god, a demonic entity represented by a man with a goat head. As you know, goats will eat anything, including metal cans and rotten garbage. This is the demonic god that ruled over Esau's descendants because of what was in their souls.

HEALING YOUR FOOD ADDICTIONS

Esau's story doesn't have to be yours. If you have soul wounds that have been passed down to you from a parent or other relative in your family line and that are manifesting in the form of food addictions or weight issues, you can be healed in the same way you can from any other soul wound. As you apply the remedies of the finished work of Christ, the cross, the blood, and dunamis power to your soul man, you will no longer need to eat for comfort. Rather, you will eat for enjoyment and to nourish your body. The obsession with food will no longer control you. You will lose weight if you need to, and the diet and exercise plan you are following will finally work. The pounds will come off and stay off. I have seen people lose as much as sixty pounds supernaturally in an instant. Others lost weight overnight, while some shed pounds like crazy as the weeks went by. The exciting thing is the weight came off after their souls were healed.

I heard from a woman who had been listening to my soul-healing messages. While she was practicing the teaching, the Holy Spirit revealed to her that she had an almost lifelong sugar addiction. When she was young, her parents divorced, and she began to use sugary foods to suppress the anxiety and fear she was experiencing. That developed a habit she continued for more than twenty years. After she started commanding her soul to be filled with dunamis, she was completely set free. Within a couple of months she had lost almost twenty pounds without doing any vigorous exercise because her soul was healed and she was no longer eating sugar.

I have also seen some incredible healings in my meetings from eating disorders such as anorexia, bulimia, and bingeing. While doing a meeting in a women's prison, I met an inmate who was suffering from two of these conditions. The first night I saw her, I was walking by the front row of female inmates when she yelled out, "Pray for my bulimia and anorexia!" I stopped and looking right at her said, "In the name of Jesus, your soul is healed, and you are free of that disease!"

The next day she came up to testify that the arthritis pain in her hips, knees, and hands that she had suffered from for many years was totally gone. She said she didn't have to take any of her pain medicine when she woke up that morning, and there were also no noises coming from her joints, as there normally would be. She believed she was also healed of the anorexia and bulimia she had suffered from for many years because she was hungry. Previously she would not have felt hungry because of the food disorders.

PRAYER ACTIVATION

Say these prayers and decrees with me, and take communion
while you do it.

> *Lord, I repent for fellowshipping and being a partner
> with demon spirits by eating at their feasts. Every
> time I sinned by overeating is now under the pow-
> erful blood of Jesus Christ. Jesus came to destroy
> the works of the devil, so I speak to any spirit that
> is on assignment to drive me to eat, and I say, "I
> will not listen to your voice. I am not hungry. I eat
> only what my body needs to be completely nour-
> ished. I resist you, Satan, so you must flee."*
>
> *I also repent for drinking the bitter water that
> causes the curse. I decree that Jesus died for every
> sin of bitterness I have ever committed. I put
> the blood of Jesus on every bitter thought, every
> bitter word, and every bitter action. I receive the
> cleansing power of the blood now, in Jesus's name.*
>
> *I decree that the power of the cross can go back
> in time through my ancestral line to wash away any
> sins related to food. I believe that when Jesus shed
> His blood on the cross, it was for the redemption of
> all the sins in my family. I release the power of the
> blood right now to cleanse my bloodline and wipe
> out all food-related sins all the way back to Adam.*
>
> *Now I put the dunamis that's in me to work so I
> can experience above and beyond all I could ever
> ask or imagine. I decree that dunamis is healing me
> of all trauma that drove me to eat. I command it to
> flow into my unhealthy appetites so I can become*

excellent of soul. I decree that dunamis is healing me of all generational issues that were passed down through my bloodline. I believe I am being strengthened and reinforced with mighty power in my inner man right now.

Jesus used His anointing of dunamis power to heal all who were oppressed of the devil [Acts 10:38]. So I decree that I am healed of all demon oppression by the dunamis anointing flowing in me. I release it into my soul and body to totally heal me. I also declare I am not a descendant of Esau, so I am not controlled by the goat god! I am a descendant of Abraham in the family of Christ, so I am free from all demonic control. As I take this communion, I decree I am fellowshipping and partnering with the body and blood of Jesus Christ and not with demon spirits by eating at their feasts. In Jesus's name, amen.

Now use the following decree to break the curse of the bitter water off your life so your belly will stop swelling and you will lose weight.

I decree that Jesus became a curse for me because the Bible says cursed is anyone who hangs on a tree [Gal. 3:13]. So right now I partake of the work He already accomplished on the cross. I command the curse of the bitter water to be broken off my life by the power of Jesus's name! I command all swelling in my belly and body to go now, and I command all unnecessary water and fat cells to dissolve and be removed from my body. I decree that I will lose

*excess weight, lose it rapidly, and never gain it back
again. In Jesus's name, amen.*

Some issues in the soul are deeply embedded. If you don't
see immediate results, don't be concerned; just prayerfully
repeat these decrees until change occurs. I also highly suggest
you use my teaching resources *Live Free: Escaping the Trap of
Bitterness of Soul* and *Soul Food.* These teachings are powerful
and will equip you to totally break through in these areas.

Chapter 11

CHARACTER BENTS

Y OUR CHARACTER IS a sum of your personality traits and beliefs. The ideal character for every person, of course, is the character of Jesus Christ. Romans 8:29 tells us that God has predestined us—which is another way of saying "pre-designed" us—to be conformed to the image of His Son. Jesus is the role model for how we should behave on a daily basis.

A person who has the character of Christ displays the fruit of the Spirit. Paul described the evidence of this fruit in Galatians 5:22–23—"love, joy, peace, longsuffering, kindness, goodness, faithfulness, gentleness, self-control." Unfortunately, though we all may aspire to develop and then consistently reflect this type of character, we usually don't.

A character bent is a behavior that causes a person to react negatively—poorly, badly, ineffectively—to situations, circumstances, and people. A person with a bent in his character will respond to his daily challenges in ways that are destructive to himself and others. Some examples of character bents are bitterness, stubbornness, rebellion, anger, and a critical and judgmental spirit. Chronic anxiety, worry, and fearfulness are character bents as well. You'll notice that these lists include issues we've referred to in previous chapters as sins that not only create soul wounds but also are then displayed by people who are wounded.

A character bent is more than a temporary fall from grace; it defines how we behave on a regular basis. Every person has some type of bent that needs straightening out in order to come into perfect alignment with the character of Christ. Ask yourself what your bents are. Then face the fact that they are probably the biggest problem you are dealing with in your life. Why?

CHARACTER BENTS ARE DESTRUCTIVE

Character bents are responsible for destroying every part of our existence. Have you ever heard a recently divorced person explain why the separation happened? The reason nearly always involves character bents. "Oh, I just couldn't stay with him anymore. He was so negative about everything. He criticized all I did and also acted the same way to the children. He never gave them any positive encouragement but was always angry at them. It got so bad that we had to leave."

Character bents destroy everything in their paths, including businesses. Maybe you've heard a person explain why he left his job. "I just couldn't work for that company any longer. The owner was a liar and a cheat. He never kept his word. He never did what he said he was going to do for us or for our customers. His behavior got so bad that he lost three very talented employees in just the last two months!"

Character bents are also responsible for destroying ministries and splitting up churches. I am sure you have heard a disgruntled layperson say something to this effect: "The pastor was too judgmental, always pointing out everybody else's sins but never examining himself," or "The leadership has a religious spirit. They spend most of their time trying to control the church instead of letting the Holy Spirit flow through it."

If you think about it, the more you listen to the complaints that drive a person away from something or someone, the more likely you are to hear a list of character bents that go along with those complaints. Bents are everywhere. They alienate us from one another, give rise to strife, and cause God's plans and purposes not to come to pass in our lives.

Character bents can also affect a person's ability to prosper. Let's say you have a bent of fear or worry, and then you lose your job. You will probably respond to that situation out of fear and panic. "Oh my gosh, what am I going to do? This is the end! I won't be able to pay this month's mortgage. I'm going to lose the house. I had better stop tithing, or I won't have enough money to pay next month's bills." The character bent of fear will not only torment you but also squash your faith. Fear always negates faith. Yet faith is what you need to make something supernatural happen in your finances.

CHARACTER BENTS MAKE US SICK

Character bents can even make you physically sick. The man Jesus healed who had an infirmity for thirty-eight years is a great example (John 5). From the meaning of the word *infirmity* we have discovered that it was his soul that made him sick.

However, it was habitual sin that caused him to be wounded in the first place. After he was healed, Jesus told him to stop sinning, or something worse would happen to him (v. 14). In a previous chapter I shared that I felt this man's sin was offense. He was upset because he didn't have any family or friends to help him into the pool. I believe he was also offended at all the other sick people who were waiting for the angel to stir the water. He told Jesus that they all would cut in front of him before he could get in the pool to get healed.

Offense is a major character bent if it is chronic. The man

by the pool was sick for thirty-eight years, which tells me in his case it was chronic. Can't you just hear Jesus saying to him, "Stop being offended, or something worse may happen to you!" Well, the Lord is telling us the exact same thing. Character bents are causing the body of Christ to be physically sick. Next time you want to blow up because someone offended you, think twice. Venting your anger at that moment might feel good, but later on you will experience the consequences of that character bent of offense in your physical body.

CHARACTER BENTS ALLOW DEMONIC SPIRITS TO ATTACK US

Bents live in the realm of the soul. They manifest as negative thoughts in your mind and are expressed through unbalanced emotions. Character bents not only control how you feel and act but also open the door for demonic oppression. I am not exaggerating when I say that almost every time I have let myself violently express my anger, a demonic spirit has immediately assaulted me.

Attitude problems are an open door for Satan, and there is a specific type of spirit that rules over these bents. It's the spirit of the giants! The Bible teaches that once there were giants in the world, and they were the enemies of God's people (Gen. 6:4). They are still around today in the form of demonic spirits, and they are on assignment to destroy you. The giants are bringers of poverty, devastation, terminal disease, and even death. But the scariest thing of all is the fact that they get their right to attack you through your "everyday" attitude problems.

Let me prove it to you. All my life I was ruled by the character bent of bitterness, which I expressed through anger. On the streets everything and everyone made me fiercely angry. My daily goal was to get back at anyone who did something

I didn't like. I was possessed by these two emotions. In fact, I can rarely remember feeling any joy except for the twisted bliss I got from hurting others.

Even as a believer, I was in bondage to my bent of bitterness and the anger that was fueled by it. I vividly recall one instance in which I was meeting with my ministry staff, and I was like a cauldron seething with anger. There we were—engaged in a powerful and effective Christian ministry, seeking God's direction, desiring His blessings—and somebody brought up something that upset me. I erupted in an angry tirade, spewing my bitterness and anger all over that conference room, all the while apologizing as I did it. I knew what I was doing was wrong, but it was as if I couldn't stop myself.

One day I became so viciously angry about something that I cried out to God for help. He gave me a vision of a standing rack for coffee cups (a mug tree) sitting on my kitchen counter with coffee mugs hanging from it. At the end of each arm was the head of a giant.

Wide-eyed, I asked God what He was trying to tell me.

Then I started looking up the words for the objects in the vision. I saw a comment about coffee that said it sometimes tasted like bitter water. When I saw those words, instantly God spoke, "You're drinking the bitter water. In fact, you are drinking mugs full of it, and it's allowing the giants [demonic spirits] to attack you."

I knew it was true; I was still being controlled by bitterness. But I wasn't sure what it had to do with giants. So I asked a friend of mine how the giants and bitterness are connected. He told me that bitterness isn't just a sin; it's a character bent. His reply helped me understand that certain sins actually have the power to bend our souls toward negative behaviors, but I still didn't understand what it had to do with the giants.

So I decided to look up the word *bent* in the Bible and was stunned at what I found. The first place it is used is in Genesis 6, which details the first appearance of the giants on the earth:

> Now giants were upon the earth in those days. For after the sons of God went in to the daughters of men, and they brought forth children, these are the mighty men of old, men of renown. And God seeing that the wickedness of men was great on the earth, and that *all the thought of their heart was bent on evil* at all times, it repented him that he made man on the earth. And being touched inwardly with sorrow of heart, He said: I will destroy man, whom I have created, from the face of the earth, from man even to beasts, from the creeping thing even to the fowls of the air, for it repenteth me I made them.
>
> —GENESIS 6:4–7, DRA, EMPHASIS ADDED

The word "heart" here is the Hebrew word *leb*, which, as we learned previously, means "the soul."[1] According to this scripture, something happened to the hearts of men when the giants appeared on the earth. Men's souls became *bent* on doing evil. Why? The giants were beings filled with all kinds of wickedness. They were combative and warlike. They worshipped idols and engaged in witchcraft and astrology (1 Sam. 17:43). In fact, outside historical sources claim that the giants taught these sinful behaviors to men, and the results were that the souls of men became bent toward evil.[2] I am sure these bents included dangerous and destructive behaviors, such as bitterness, rebellion, stubbornness, and the like. The giants' influence on men was so great that it brought about the destruction of every person on earth except Noah and his immediate family!

The Bible says in 2 Peter 2:5 that the Lord brought the flood upon the world of the ungodly. Because of the bent condition of men's souls there was not one person left on earth who was righteous. The hearts of all the people were so poisoned that every man, woman, and child had to be destroyed. That is how devastating character bents can be.

Here's the worst part: these bents weren't eliminated when the giants were killed in the deluge. Rather, the Bible says the giants existed both *before and after* the flood (Gen. 6:4).

Although they were wiped out in the deluge, the spirits of the giants continued to manifest in men of gigantic size in Canaan. By the time the Israelites entered the Land of Promise, giants had repopulated the land. Canaan was riddled with them. Goliath and his brothers were just a few examples.

When the armies of Israel marched into Canaan, they faced one of the ancient world's fiercest giants, Og, king of Bashan, who ruled over a tribe of giant people. We know he was huge because the Bible says his bed was fourteen feet long (Deut. 3:11)! The Amorites, another tribe of giants, also resided in Canaan. According to the biblical account, they were as tall as the cedars and as strong as the oaks (Amos 2:9). The list of giants in the land goes on and on. They were everywhere.

They had resurged into the earth and were doing the same things they had done before. They were agents of pure evil who taught mankind how to worship idols, make blood sacrifices to false gods, perform the tricks of witchcraft, and engage in practices associated with the occult (1 Sam. 17:43, KJV).[3] They imparted to men and women the desire to engage in all types of sins that *bent* men's hearts toward evil and away from God.

Believe it or not, the spirits of the giants are still active today, and their work is the same as it always was. They are intent on bending our hearts toward all that God prohibits and abhors, and many times the fruit of that bending is the bad behaviors in your life that destroy your marriage, family, health, and prosperity. This world is full of offended, angry, bitter, critical, and rebellious people. No wonder Jesus said the end times would be like the days of Noah!

A KING WITH CHARACTER BENTS

When I asked the Lord to show me someone in the Bible who had character bents that came from the giants, He immediately replied, "King Saul!" Saul had failed to defeat the Philistines, who were led by giants. The reason for his defeat was because he had something in his soul that was in common with them—his character bents.

Saul's downfall began when God commanded Saul through the prophet Samuel to destroy King Agag (1 Sam. 15:3). Samuel was the high priest, so it was his job to speak the word of the Lord to God's leaders, including the king. The Lord wanted Saul to destroy King Agag, all his people, and all their livestock (v. 3). But Saul didn't obey God's command to the letter; he and his people "spared Agag, and the best of the sheep, and of the oxen, and of the fatlings, and the lambs, and all that was good, and would not utterly destroy them" (v. 9). As a result, Samuel chastised him. He told Saul that his rebellion was as the sin of witchcraft and his stubbornness as idolatry (v. 23). Rebellion and stubbornness are serious character bents!

Where did Saul acquire these bents? I believe the answer lies in 1 Samuel 9, which opens with the genealogy of Saul's family:

> There was a man of Benjamin whose name was Kish the son of Abiel, the son of Zeror, the son of Bechorath, the son of Aphiah, a Benjamite, a mighty man of power.
>
> —1 SAMUEL 9:1

Saul's father, Kish, was called a "mighty man," which is the same phrase used in Genesis 6 to describe the giants who were the mighty men of old. Now guess what the name *Kish* means? It is the Hebrew word *Qiysh*, which means "bent"![4]

Saul inherited his character bents from his father. Interestingly Kish's father, who was Saul's grandfather, was named "Abiel." One of the root words of his name in Hebrew is 'el, which can mean "mighty men," "angels," "false god," or "demons."[5]

After the Bible details Saul's genealogy, it tells us Saul was the most handsome man in Israel and that he stood head and shoulders taller than anyone else in the land (1 Sam. 9:2). I'm not implying that all tall people are giants, but I find it interesting that Saul was of such great stature compared to the people of his same nationality. To me, it is further proof of the giant influence in his life.

THE INFLUENCE OF GIANTS IN MY LIFE

I believe that, like Saul, I had "mighty men" (in the biblical sense I've been referring to) in my bloodline. Their influence manifested in many different ways, from character bents to unusual strength. I am not a large person, but I used to be able to lift objects many times my size. Once when I was helping my aunt move her furniture, I walked into her living room, threw her love seat up on my shoulder, and walked with it into the other room. For someone with my stature that would be impossible unless a giant spirit (or an angel) was helping. I can guarantee you that in my case it wasn't an angel!

Suddenly, a few years back I lost all my strength. I couldn't even walk up a set of stairs unless I took one stair at a time with breaks in between. I had been very strong my whole life, so the change was alarming, and I had no idea what had brought it about. I soon found out.

One day while on tour I was in my hotel room getting

dressed and happened to see myself in the full-length mirror on the closet doors. (I didn't have a full-length mirror in my house.) I was shocked! My thighs were totally emaciated. I had long indentations in my legs where the muscles had atrophied, and there was loose skin hanging off my thighs because of the loss of muscle mass. I was undone. No wonder I had felt so weak.

The next day while on the plane, I asked God to tell me what was wrong. He immediately said "Numbers 5" and showed me a vision of a glass of iced tea. When I looked it up, I found the definition of the word *tea* to be "an aromatic, slightly bitter beverage."[6] That's when the Lord gently said, "You're still drinking the bitter water."

The scripture I heard was Numbers 5:24, which refers to the priest's having a woman accused of being unfaithful "drink the bitter water that brings a curse." If the woman was guilty, the water caused her belly to swell and *her thigh to rot* (v. 27). I was drinking the bitter water, and my thigh was rotting because of it.

At that moment I realized the character bent of bitterness could make people lose their strength and suffer muscle atrophy. I can't tell you how many times since I received this revelation I have asked attendees in my meetings if they have an unexplained loss of strength and are also bitter for some reason. Hundreds have raised their hands. Even more startling is the fact that it is the spirits of the giants that are behind these attacks. In Numbers 5:27 the word for "rot" is the Hebrew word *naphal*, which is the root of *nĕphiyl*. The way it is written in English is *nephilim*, which is another word for "giants" that is used in Genesis 6:4.[7] This proves that the cancers, weight gain, and thigh rot that come from the character bent of bitterness have their origins in these giant spirits.

When I repented of my bitterness and released dunamis in

my soul, my muscles grew back within a month with no exercise at all!

In one meeting after I had taught about the giants and bitterness, we were all praying for dunamis to heal our souls when a man started screaming and jumping up and down. Later he told me that he had been a bitter person his whole life. His character bent was devastating his marriage and his children. He added that in the last year or two he had unexplainably lost his strength. He became so weak that he was unable to exercise or do anything. The doctors couldn't pinpoint the cause.

While we were praying, he felt a spirit lift off him, and when it did, all the bitter feelings in his soul left and his body became completely energized. The next day he was smiling from ear to ear and said he felt as if he were twenty years old again!

A friend of mine came to my house one day to "soak" in the presence of the Lord. After we were finished worshipping, she showed me a fist-sized hole in her thigh. She said the doctors had no idea what was causing the extreme amount of muscle atrophy, but I did. It was thigh rot from bitterness. Over a period of months we worked on it together, and the hole completely filled in with no exercise at all.

HOW DO WE GET CHARACTER BENTS?

The good news is that a lot of these character bents are your parents' fault! The bents Saul had in his soul were passed down to him through his bloodline. It may be that the same attitude problems your parents had, you have too. Soul wounds can be passed down from one family member to the next. These generational iniquities, as David called them, get formed in your soul while you are being fashioned in the womb. Interestingly enough, the root of the word "iniquity" in Hebrew is the word `avah, which means "to bend"![8] That's how powerful these generational wounds are. They have the power to bend your soul toward evil, creating character bents inside your inner man that can devastate your life.

DUNAMIS HEALS YOU OF YOUR BENTS

Often you hear people being described according to the bents in their personalities. For example, "I don't like hanging out with him because he is so mean and rude," or "She is so inconsiderate to everyone around her that I would rather not be her friend."

How do people describe *your* personality? Before I was healed, I would have been labeled as "mean," "irate," and "volatile." Now I believe people would give me a different report. I have heard words such as "faithful," "tenacious," "loyal," and even "loving" used to describe my personality. I believe these words reflect more accurately what I am like now because I have called on the dunamis power of God to heal me of the bents in my soul.

Look again at Paul's prayer in Ephesians 3:16 (AMPC):

> May He grant you out of the rich treasury of His glory to be strengthened and reinforced with mighty power [dunamis] in the inner man by the [Holy] Spirit [Himself indwelling your innermost being and personality].

Paul asks that God's mighty power of dunamis not only strengthen and reinforce your inner man but also indwell your personality because of the presence of the Holy Spirit! That means dunamis has the power to heal you of all the character bents that are controlling your personality and then cause the power of the giants to be broken off your life. I have overcome the bitter bent in my soul by battling against it with the blood and dunamis. When I used to feel bitterness rise up in me, I would decree:

- I am the righteousness of God in Christ.

- My sins are already forgiven.

- I am full of dunamis.

- It strengthens and reinforces my inner man and my personality.

- I don't have a bitter character.

- I possess a joyful personality because dunamis is making me excellent of soul.

- I am a positive person.

- I am peaceful.

- I am not bitter, angry, upset, critical, or judgmental because dunamis is flowing into my personality right now, healing me and making me excellent of soul!

A WOMAN WHO BECAME EXCELLENT OF SOUL

When I asked the Lord to show me a character in the Bible who had mighty men in his or her bloodline but was healed by dunamis, I was shocked to hear Him name Mary, the mother of Jesus.

We know Jesus had to be born without spot or blemish so He could be the atoning sacrifice for all mankind (1 Pet. 1:19). This means He had to be perfect in all three parts of His being, including having no wounds in His soul. Clearly He would have received no soul issues from His Father, God. But what about from Mary? She wasn't divine but rather human, like you and me.

Some people believe that Mary was born sinless. But that's impossible because the Bible says *all* have sinned and fallen short of the glory of God.

Even if Mary had not transgressed in her lifetime, it is unreasonable to think that everyone in her bloodline, all the way back to Adam, was also sinless. Thus she must have been born with the junk her ancestors had in their souls. If this is true, how could she have become the mother of Jesus? The wounds in her inner being would have been passed down to Jesus while He was being formed in her womb.

What happened? The angel Gabriel made it clear. When he told her the shocking news that she was going to become pregnant even though she had not been intimate with a man, and she asked how this could be since she was a virgin (Luke 1:30–34), the angel replied: "The Holy Spirit will come upon you, and the power of the Most High will overshadow you" (Luke 1:35, AMP). Not surprisingly the word "power" here is the word dunamis! When Holy Spirit overshadowed Mary, He not only caused her to conceive supernaturally but also made her excellent of soul.

Mary wasn't born sinless, but she was made pure by a visitation of dunamis so she could be fit to be the mother of our Savior. When dunamis overshadowed her, it healed her of everything in her soul that she would have passed down to her Son.

Let me prove this truth through additional verses. Look at what Mary said about how she felt after she was overshadowed by God's power:

> My soul magnifies the Lord, and my spirit has rejoiced
> in God my Savior. For He has regarded the lowly state of
> His maidservant.
> —Luke 1:46–48

Notice Mary's *soul* magnified the Lord. Why? She must have felt like a new person. Dunamis had overshadowed her and made her excellent of soul! Trust me, when you have been healed by dunamis, you can feel it in your mind, will, emotions, and entire being.

But how do I know for sure that Mary was talking about her soul being healed? Because she declared, "He has regarded the lowly state of His maidservant" (v. 48).

The phrase "lowly estate" here is the Greek word *tapeinōsis*, which means "leading one to perceive and lament his (moral) littleness and guilt."[9] Out of her own mouth Mary confessed the moral guilt she had been carrying in her inner man before God's dunamis power overshadowed her. Mary wasn't born perfect. She was made pure and excellent of soul by a visitation of dunamis so she could be totally fit to conceive and carry Jesus!

I wept when I read this. If she could be healed by one visitation of dunamis, then there is no limit to what can happen to us! We have dunamis inside of us 24/7!

I often wondered what Mary needed to be healed of. I got my answer as I continued reading the text. After Mary said that her soul magnified the Lord, she went on to make this shocking statement:

> He has put down the *mighty* from their thrones!
> —Luke 1:52, AMPC, EMPHASIS ADDED

Mary had "mighty" in her genealogy! She, like almost every other person on the planet, had giant influences in her soul.

Yet when dunamis healed her, those mighty men were thrown down from their positions of power in her bloodline!

PRAYER ACTIVATION

If you are dealing with generational issues and character bents that have taken on "giant" size in your life, place your hands on your belly and make this declaration:

> I have dunamis power in me. My soul is becoming excellent. I don't care if I have been like Saul, with a father who passed down many character bents. My soul is magnifying the Lord, for He has thrown down the mighty from their thrones.
>
> I don't care if I have mighty men in my bloodline. The character bents that came from them are being destroyed, and my soul is magnifying the Lord, for He has thrown down the mighty from their thrones.
>
> It doesn't matter if my relatives have passed on to me the traits of being stubborn, rebellious, bitter, or afraid. It doesn't matter that they have passed on to me traits of being depressed or anxious. I now have dunamis power flowing in me, and it is healing my personality. My soul is magnifying the Lord, for He has thrown down the mighty from their thrones.
>
> I declare to the wounds that are connected to the giants in my bloodline that I am healed, overshadowed, and filled with dunamis so my soul magnifies the Lord—for He has thrown down the mighty from their thrones. In Jesus's name, amen!

If you are praying for another person, lay hands on him or her and declare:

> *You are being healed by dunamis power. Your soul is going to magnify the Lord. The mighty are being thrown from their thrones. You are not like Saul. It doesn't matter if there have been giants in your bloodline. All your character bents are being removed, and your personality is healed because of the power of Christ Jesus.*

You are displaying all the fruit of the spirit because dunamis is flowing into your entire being. You are full of love, joy, peace, longsuffering, kindness, goodness, faithfulness, gentleness, and self-control. You are being made excellent of soul by the dunamis power surging through you right now! In Jesus's name, amen!

Chapter 12

STAYING FREE

Y OU'VE LEARNED A lot in this book about healing a
wounded soul. But I would be remiss if I didn't tell you
about two of the most powerful weapons I use in soul healing
and in helping people remain free after they are healed: worship and the snow and hail. Both have a foundation in Scripture, as you will see. Worship is very effective at facilitating
healing, helping us to hear from God, and rebuking the
enemy from our lives, while snow and hail defeat evil spirits—
particularly the spirits of Legion and the giants.

WORSHIP HEALS THE SOUL

When Jesus was on the earth, He gave His disciples what He
called the first and greatest commandment: "And thou shalt
love the Lord thy God with all thy heart, and with all thy
soul, and with all thy mind, and with all thy strength" (Mark
12:30, KJV).

Worship is a powerful way to fulfill this command. When
you set aside every desire in your heart and every thought dis-
tracting your mind to worship God, you are loving your heavenly Father with all that you are. This abandoning of the soul
causes a holy exchange—your junk for His majesty—which
results in intimate relationship and massive inner healing.

True worship is a sacrifice that requires lavishly giving your time, spiritual gifts, and resources to the Lord. It is not sufficient to worship Him for just one hour one day a week, on Sundays. Real worshippers live a lifestyle of worship. And though it demands something of us to offer up a "sacrifice of praise" (Heb. 13:15), it is worth the cost.

Every time I forgo my busyness to get in His presence, I receive much in return. In fact, the number one thing that has positioned me to be healed in my soul, have a highly successful ministry, and work mighty miracles has been my faithfulness to worship God day after day, week after week, and year after year. The times when I was inconsistent, I would get sick, have financial trouble, and see fewer miracles in my life and in my meetings.

Exciting things always happen in the presence of God that don't occur anywhere else. Soul healing is one of them. The Bible says that as we behold God's glory, we are transformed by the Spirit of the Lord into His image and likeness (2 Cor. 3:18). Worship ushers His glory into our atmosphere then changes us to look more like Him. As we get in His presence, His glory fills the room and brings soul-healing power with it. Worship is probably the most powerful thing you can do in your pursuit of God and the healing of your wounds.

However, there are times when what's in your soul will try to block you from worshipping. At these moments it's important for you to press through the resistance. Otherwise you will be right where the enemy wants you: wounded and at his mercy.

King David knew how to press in regardless of his difficult circumstances. He would command his soul to praise God.

> Bless the LORD, O my soul: and all that is within me,
> bless his holy name. Bless the LORD, O my soul, and

forget not all his benefits: Who forgiveth all thine iniquities; who healeth all thy diseases.

—PSALM 103:1–3, KJV

David broke through in worship by repeatedly making
himself bless the Lord. The results were that his soul was
blessed and his generational iniquities and physical diseases
were healed!

Sometimes you need to *command* your soul to bless God
because your inner man will not always feel like pursuing
Him. Yet if you overcome your resistance and bring a sacrifice
of praise, you will experience great fruit. When I am having
a hard time getting into His presence, I sing along to a worship song. By simply opening your mouth and raising your
voice, you can overcome the opposition to worship that is in
your soul.

Also, it helps to take action in your worship. David leaped
and whirled before the Lord (2 Sam. 6:14, 16). Keep engaged
by singing, raising your hands, praying in your spiritual language, waving banners, reading Scripture out loud, or whatever the Lord puts on your heart. I do all these things until
I feel the resistance break. Then often I just lie in God's presence, resting in His goodness. Sometimes I even take a nap,
and when I wake up, I am often healed in soul and body!

WORSHIP OPENS US UP TO REVELATION

Worship dispels the confusion and lack of knowledge that
often overcome us and opens our minds to receive revelation.
When the cloud of God's glory appeared on the Mount of
Transfiguration, the disciples had an encounter that revealed
Jesus and the Father to them.

Jesus took Peter, James, and John and led them up a high mountain. His appearance changed from the inside out, right before their eyes. His clothes shimmered, glistening white, whiter than any bleach could make them. Elijah, along with Moses, came into view, in deep conversation with Jesus. Peter interrupted, "Rabbi, this is a great moment! Let's build three memorials—one for you, one for Moses, one for Elijah." He blurted this out without thinking, stunned as they all were by what they were seeing. Just then a light-radiant cloud enveloped them, and from deep in the cloud, a voice: "This is my Son, marked by my love. Listen to him."

—MARK 9:2–7, THE MESSAGE

At first the disciples were totally clueless about what was going on. Yet because of the presence of the glory cloud everything changed. Their eyes were opened, and they saw what no human being had witnessed before—Jesus in His full glory. They also got to hear the voice of the Father as He imparted to them the most significant revelation anyone could receive: "This is my Son, marked by my love. Listen to him" (v. 7).

When you are in the presence of the glory of God through worship, you will receive indescribable insights into the secrets and mysteries of God and all He has for you. Mark 9:6 says that the disciples were "stunned" by what they were seeing. I have had the same reaction during worship, which is when I have received most of the revelations I teach about the wounded soul. I know these insights are from God because they have transformed the lives of countless people around the world.

In God's presence you will also receive understanding about things that are going on in your life or inside you. There is nothing worse than being in the midst of a battle or a difficult situation and not having a clue about why it's happening or what to do about it. As you worship, you will receive revelation from the Holy Spirit that will bring soul healing, solve problems, and shut down the enemy. When you worship, God speaks. The atmosphere in your home and in your soul (mind, will, and emotions) is cleared out, and glory fills you instead. When that happens, you can perceive what the Lord is communicating so you can get your breakthrough.

WAYS GOD COMMUNICATES DURING WORSHIP

God wants you to have the healing and the answers you need. When you are in His presence, He will often download insights to help you get them. For example, He may cause a word or a Scripture reference to pop into your spirit. When He does, look up the word or reference in the Bible, and meditate on the entire chapter it is contained in. As you reflect on what you heard, the Holy Spirit will give you even more detail so you can understand what He is trying to say to you.

Make sure you write down everything you are hearing, sensing, and seeing. At first it might seem unclear, but the more you read, research, and record your insights, the more the revelation will increase. Then when the Holy Spirit is done speaking, decree the scriptures and revelations you received over your situation. The Bible says if you decree a thing, it will be established as the light shines on all your ways (Job 22:28).

Another way God communicates is through dreams and visions. Worship will cause the realm of dreams and visions to open up. When you receive a vision or dream, look up the meanings of everything you saw, using the Bible and a dictionary as your main sources for doing research. You will likely find that the symbols in your dreams will lead you to a chapter in the Bible, which is God's intent. The Word holds the revelation of God. In it is everything you need for every issue you face.

Once I was fiercely battling a spirit that was making me physically ill. After a couple of weeks of struggling, I saw a vision of a train rolling down a track. When I asked God what it meant, He said, "Look it up in your Bible." I couldn't recall ever reading anything about trains in the Bible, so I was skeptical, but He was insistent. When I put the word *train* in the word search of my electronic Bible, an insightful verse came up:

> You have ascended on high. You have led away captive a train of vanquished foes; You have received gifts of men, yes, of the rebellious also, that the Lord God might dwell there with them.
> —PSALM 68:18, AMPC

Through the symbol of a train the Lord showed me that He had already vanquished my foes. I was delivered! The illness in my body left immediately, and I was healed. (For more information on how to interpret your dreams and visions, get my healing resource *Interpreting Dreams and Visions for Your Soul*.)

WORSHIP IS WARFARE

Worship is a form of spiritual warfare. When you lift up your voice to God, you shake demons off every part of your life. This is good news, considering that we battle with them regularly:

> For we wrestle not against flesh and blood, but against… the rulers of the darkness of this world, against spiritual wickedness in high places.
> —EPHESIANS 6:12, KJV

This verse says we "wrestle" against demonic powers. So how do we win the match? Through worship! The word "wrestle" is the Greek word *pale*, which means "to vibrate."[1] When you sing, praise, and lift up your voice to God, you vibrate with the heavenly frequencies of worship. If you vibrate enough, you will shake off everything that is sticking to you, including a demonic spirit. Worship is one way you wrestle against the enemy. It is a powerful tool against Satan.

The Bible contains many examples that prove praise and worship defeat our foes. One of them is the account of when a great multitude came against King Jehoshaphat and the people in Jerusalem. After the people of God fasted, the Bible says the spirit of the Lord came upon the prophets of the land with this message.

> Be not afraid or dismayed at this great multitude; for the battle is not yours, but God's....You shall not need to fight in this battle; take your positions, stand still, and see the deliverance of the Lord.
>
> —2 CHRONICLES 20:15, 17, AMPC

After hearing the prophetic word of victory, Jehoshaphat appointed singers to go before the army as they marched out to sing praises to the Lord. Then as the people sang, the Lord set ambushments against their enemies, who turned against one another then were self-slaughtered. Afterward Jehoshaphat and his people took so much cattle, goods, garments, and precious stones that had been left behind that it took three days for them to gather the spoils! (See 2 Chronicles 20:18–25.)

As you pursue soul healing, the power that is in worship will not only heal your soul but also drive the enemy to let go of you and even destroy itself while you are left with piles of bounty and treasure.

You will be amazed at how much healing and deliverance you will receive through your times of praise and worship. Consider the account of the Israelites' defeat of the Assyrians.

> At the voice of the Lord the Assyrians will be stricken with dismay and terror, when He smites them with His rod. And every passing stroke of the staff of punishment and doom which the Lord lays upon them shall be to the sound of [Israel's] timbrels and lyres, when in battle He attacks [Assyria] with swinging and menacing arms.
> —Isaiah 30:31–32, AMPC

This account encourages us to believe that the Lord will defeat our enemies through our worship. As we sing, praise, and play music to the Lord, He whacks the devils that are attacking us with His "swinging and menacing arms" (v. 32). They are defeated to the beat of our songs!

Worship is one of the greatest tools God has given me to defeat the enemy. Countless times I have been delivered of a demonic spirit as I praised the Lord.

Over the years I have noticed a pattern for the way healing takes place in my life. Clearly this is not the only way; the Holy Spirit will use many different approaches. However, this is one way I found to be very successful in my personal life.

- I get hit with a sickness.

- During worship the Holy Spirit tells me what caused the attack (usually a soul wound) and what evil spirit is attacking me. Sometimes the revelation comes in a dream or a vision during or after worship.

- I make soul-healing decrees based on the Word of God.

- I keep worshipping day after day, and the power to heal builds up.

- God heals my soul wound, and the demonic spirit that is attached to it comes off, taking his sickness with him. Often this happens during worship or after worship in the night while I sleep. (See my resource *Miracles in the Night* for more information.)

I have seen this pattern at work in my life more times than I can count, and the result is that I have been healed of all kinds of ailments—from cancer to terrible symptoms associated with menopause to invasion of my body by viruses and bacteria of many kinds.

I often follow a similar "format" during my meetings, though I am always open to the direction of the Holy Spirit:

- I start by teaching on soul healing to build faith in people to get their breakthrough.

- I lead everyone through prayers that will help them begin to get healed.

- I bring everyone up to the altar to worship so the dunamis glory can continue the healing process.

- I wait for the Holy Spirit to tell me when people are healed; then I command spirits to leave and take their curses and diseases with them.

- As I ask people to check for a new level of peace in their souls and test their bodies, physical healings begin to manifest throughout the room.

I have seen some amazing miracles happen through this simple process.

MY SECRET WEAPON FOR HEALING AND DELIVERANCE

There are secrets in the kingdom of God that, when revealed to us, can be used powerfully in our deliverance and in the continuation of our healing. Many of these secrets are not overtly revealed in Scripture but are easily seen once the believer is on the lookout for them and is being led by the Holy Spirit. However, sometimes we have to mature spiritually before we can discover and understand them. Jesus told His disciples:

> I have still many things to say to you, but you are not able to bear them or to take them upon you or to grasp them now. But when He, the Spirit of Truth (the Truth-giving Spirit) comes, He will guide you into all the Truth (the whole, full Truth).
> —John 16:12–13, AMPC

Jesus said there were many other things He wanted to teach His disciples, but they weren't ready for them yet. Thankfully He promised that the Holy Spirit would guide them—as He does us—into all those truths when the timing was right.

There are many deliverance tools I use that are unusual in their operation yet are totally scriptural. I also have uncommon signs follow me. I rarely share these things in public because I am often questioned about them. People claim that because the Scriptures don't show Jesus moving in these things, they must not be legitimate. However, the Bible makes it clear that not everything Jesus did is recorded there.

> And there are also many other things which Jesus did. If they should be all recorded one by one [in detail], I suppose that even the world itself could not contain (have room for) the books that would be written.
>
> —John 21:25, ampc

There are *countless* things Jesus did—so many the world couldn't contain the full account of them—that are not described in Scripture. Does this truth give us the right to go off the ranch and create crazy, unfounded doctrines? Absolutely not! As you will see, the supernatural tools and signs I am going to share with you have their foundation in Scripture. I will leave it to you to judge their validity according to the Word.

Snow and Hail

Years ago when I was first fighting Legion, I was totally frustrated. At that time he seemed like an overwhelming foe. I was healed of dwelling among the tombs, but even after I was, I couldn't seem to get completely free of him.

Then I had an unusual encounter with an angel. As I was praying for secrets and mysteries to be revealed to me concerning my enemy, I was taken into a vision. I saw myself sitting glumly on the curb of a street. Suddenly out of nowhere an angel driving an ice truck came roaring up next to me. He came screeching to a halt, rolled down his window, and threw a bag of ice at me. Then just as quickly he peeled out and left.

I came out of the vision dumbfounded and thought, "What in the world does that mean, God?" But one thing I have learned over the years is that I can always find my answers in the Word. I began a search of every place in Scripture that talked about ice and hail, and boy, did I get excited! There are verses and stories throughout the Bible that prove God uses snow or hail as a supernatural weapon against our enemies.

We see an amazing example of the use of hail in the story related in Joshua 10. Joshua and his men were fighting a fierce battle at Gibeon against five of the Amorite kings and their armies. They marched all night from Gilgal and then suddenly came upon the opposing armies. Amazingly they were able to rout them with a great slaughter (Josh. 10:7–10). But Joshua and his army didn't do it alone. During the battle something mind-blowing happened:

> The LORD cast down large hailstones from heaven on them as far as Azekah, and they died. There were more who died from the hailstones than the children of Israel killed with the sword.
> —JOSHUA 10:11

Out of nowhere the heavens poured out huge hailstones on Joshua's adversaries. This heavenly visitation was so spectacular that the hail killed more men than the sword! Remarkably not a single hailstone hit an Israelite warrior. Instead, the hail selectively killed only their enemies!

Numerous accounts in the Bible show that the Lord uses snow and hail to battle against our enemies. Job 38:22–23 says, "Have you entered the treasury of snow, or have you seen the treasury of hail, which I have reserved for the time of trouble, for the day of battle and war?" God stores up the snow and hail in a treasury for the day we need a weapon to battle against our enemies. After I saw in a vision an angel bring me a bag of ice, the Lord told me I had been given power to call on snow and hail and to release them against evil spirits to defeat them.

God's raining down snow and hail on our enemies is a biblical concept. A good example is the plague of hail He put on Egypt when Pharaoh wouldn't let the Israelites leave that land.

> ""Behold, tomorrow about this time I will cause very heavy hail to rain down, such as has not been in Egypt since its founding until now. Therefore send now and gather your livestock and all that you have in the field, for the hail shall come down on every man and every animal which is found in the field and is not brought home; and they shall die."" He who feared the word of the LORD among the servants of Pharaoh made his servants and his livestock flee to the houses. But he who did not regard the word of the LORD left his servants and his livestock in the field. Then the LORD said to Moses, "Stretch out your hand toward heaven, that there may be hail in all the land of Egypt—on man, on beast, and on every herb of the field, throughout the land of Egypt." And Moses stretched out his rod toward heaven; and the LORD sent thunder and hail, and fire darted to the ground. And the LORD rained hail on the land of Egypt. So there was hail, and fire mingled with the hail, so very heavy that there was none like it in all the land of Egypt since it became a nation. And the hail struck throughout the whole land of Egypt, all that was in the field, both man and beast; and the hail struck every herb of the field and broke every tree of the field.
>
> —EXODUS 9:18–25

Hailstorms were unusual in arid regions such as Egypt and were therefore extremely frightening. What made this storm even more terrorizing was that the hail was mixed with fire, making it obvious that it was of supernatural origin.

The plague of hail came against such demonic Egyptian gods as Shu, the wind god; Nut, the sky goddess; and Horus, the hawk-headed sky god of upper Egypt. Powerless, these demons were unable to stop the hail, and it laid a heavy judgment on them.

God uses the snow and hail to punish evil spirits. I can't tell you how many times I have been personally delivered from a demon through the use of this unusual weapon released in the name of Jesus.

One night at one of my meetings there was so much power in the worship that I knew I was getting some deep soul healing. Afterward when I got home, I had an encounter. As I was drifting off to sleep, I saw a vision of a heavy snowfall coming down in huge globs. I had been walking in the weapons of the snow and hail for years, so I knew something amazing was happening. Then I was taken into a deep sleep. The next morning I knew I had been delivered of something, but I wasn't sure what. However, as the days and weeks passed, it became obvious what had happened.

I was fifty-two years old at the time. Six months prior to that event I began having severe hot flashes and the types of sweats that made me smell like a trucker who hadn't bathed in a week. The sweating was so bad it left my bed soaking wet every night, even though I had a ceiling fan over me and a floor fan pointed directly at the bed. Night and day the sweats never stopped. When I was preaching, I would sometimes perspire so much and smell so bad that my assistant had to bring body spray and deodorant as well as an extra outfit for me to change into—even though I had a fan pointed at the podium the whole time.

However, since the night I had the vision of the snowfall, I have not had a single hot flash or sweating episode! Through worship and the treasury of snow and hail that is stored up for the day of battle and war, I was delivered of a demon that was causing me to experience symptoms of menopause. (Think about my experience, ladies; this means a demonic spirit causes menopause! That's a revelation many of you need right now.)

Psalm 18:13–14 says when God speaks, He releases hail to scatter His enemies:

> The LORD thundered from heaven, and the Most High uttered His voice, hailstones and coals of fire. He sent out His arrows and scattered the foe, lightnings in abundance, and He vanquished them.

According to this verse all God has to do is speak, and hailstones are released against our foes to vanquish them. The Bible also says when God decrees the destruction of our enemies, the snow and hail accomplish His word: "Fire and hail, snow and clouds; stormy wind, fulfilling His word" (Ps. 148:8, NASB).

Releasing snow and hail is one of the things I do in my meetings during the worship. It is a special mantle for deliverance the Lord has given me. While people are worshipping at the end of the session, I am usually on stage calling down hail on their enemies. The music is so loud that no one realizes what I am doing. If they heard what I was praying, they may not understand, as I have never heard of anyone else working this wonder. That's one of the reasons I decided to share it with you. I believe all God's people can employ this powerful weapon.

In fact, I use it particularly when I am fighting Legion and the giants. Each time I do, I see some amazing miracles.

LEGION IS A WATER ANIMAL

I am often asked why water comes out of people when they are delivered of Legion. To find out, let's look again at the story of the Gerasene demoniac.

When Jesus sent the spirit of Legion that had possessed the demoniac into the pigs, did that spirit remain on dry land? No, he intentionally drove the pigs into the water (Mark 5:12–13). That's because Legion is a water animal. Like any other unclean spirit, He doesn't like places that are dry and waterless.

> Now when the unclean spirit has gone out of a man, it roams through waterless (dry, arid) places in search of rest, but it does not find it. Then it says, "I will return to my house from which I came."
>
> —MATTHEW 12:43–44, AMP

This scripture gives us some very interesting insight into the preferences of demons. They don't like dry and waterless places (v. 43). (If you were bound for hellfire for eternity, you wouldn't either.) They hate them so much they can find no rest where it's dry (v. 43). This is why the unclean spirit said, "I will return to my house from which I came" (v. 44). The "house" he is referring to is a person.

Human beings are made up of up to 70 percent water.[2] Our high water content is one of the many reasons demons choose to afflict us. They love water, so we provide them with a place where they can find rest while tormenting us.

Legion is somehow able to infect the waters and bodily fluids in our bodies. This is how he spreads viruses and bacteria into our systems. Once a person gets healed of their tombs—past soul wounds they are dwelling on—and the snow and hail beat down on the head of Legion, he is driven out and takes his diseases with him.

One inmate had an unusual experience after he heard me teach on Legion and was delivered of this spirit. When he returned to his dorm after the meeting, he leaned down to take his shoes off, and as he did, water poured out of his nose—so much water that it ran down his arm and he had to use a towel to wipe it off. At the same time, he realized that he had received a physical healing and was able to stop taking pain medication for the condition. He told us that everyone in his unit knew he had been healed because he used to complain all the time about how much pain he was in.

Another inmate had just lost his mom. Even though he loved her, he didn't cry when he learned she had died because he didn't want the other inmates to see him weeping. While hearing the message on Legion, he broke down and couldn't stop crying. Later that night he woke up feeing as if he needed to throw up. He rushed to the bathroom and threw up a lot of water. Afterward he said he felt better than he ever had in his life. But he wasn't healed only of his grief. As he told me his story, I sensed the Lord telling me he had been healed of the tombs and of diverticulitis, which is a bacterium that affects the intestines. When the snow and hail hit, Legion left and took the man's disease with him.

HAILING ON THE GIANTS

Previously in this chapter we read about Joshua and his men fighting the armies of the Amorites (Josh. 10:7–10). It's important to realize that Joshua's enemies were not just ordinary human beings; they were giants. God referred to them as such through the prophet Amos: "Yet it was I who destroyed the Amorite before them, whose height was like the height of the cedars, and he was as strong as the oaks" (Amos 2:9–10). He described the Amorites as men of great stature and strength.

The Jewish historian Flavius Josephus said they had "bodies so large, and countenances so entirely different from other men, that they were surprising to the sight, and terrible to the hearing."[3]

Joshua was not battling normal humans that day but rather a nation of dangerous giant beings. Once I saw that, it made sense to me why God had used large hailstones to defeat them (Josh. 10:11). Huge balls of rock-hard ice hurled from the sky made a perfect weapon against a tribe of giants!

As I do when I am rebuking Legion in my meetings, I release hail on the giants as people are worshipping. It works! In fact, some of our most spectacular miracles—those in which metal disappears from a person's body—have occurred during these moments.

METAL MIRACLES

Many times metal is used in surgical procedures to help heal or stabilize a bone or even replace one that has been destroyed through accident, injury, or disease. What I have found is that the giants have the power to manipulate metal in people's bodies to cause them excruciating pain and limited movement. When people get healed in their souls of the character bents they have in common with the giants, many times the metal in their bodies undergoes a change. I have seen three things happen to metal in my meetings.

1. The metal remains, but the person's pain
disappears.

2. God changes the molecular form of the metal. Even though it is still there, the pain is gone, and the people can move their bodies in ways they couldn't before because of the rigidity of the metal.

3. The metal disappears and is replaced with a new body part.

One time I was in a prison teaching on character bents. After leading the men to pray for their souls to be healed by dunamis, I had them all come up to worship. During the worship time I secretly released snow and hail from the treasury in heaven.

As soon as I did this, the giants began to flee. Then the heavens opened up, and I saw angels coming down a ladder carrying new body parts.

Immediately I heard the Lord say, "Pray for people who have metal in their bodies." I gulped because I had never done it before, but I quickly obeyed. When I asked people with metal in their bodies to come forward, one man got up on the stage. He had bolts and screws in his neck from an accident. I could tell the angels were already working on him because he said his pain level had gone from a ten to a four, and the constant tightness in his neck was dissipating. I was asking God for total healing, so I prayed for his soul and then commanded the metal to disappear and be replaced with new body parts. I had him remain on stage so the angels could keep operating on him.

Then another man came up. He said while I was praying for the first man, pain suddenly shot through his body and then stopped. He had suffered from chronic pain for many years after a thirty-two-foot oil pipe fell on him, breaking his neck and back. As a result, he had undergone numerous surgeries and had an assortment of rods, plates, screws, and bolts in his neck and spine. But after the momentary flare-up in the meeting, the pain was completely gone.

I had him stand on stage while I went back to see how the first man was doing. He reported that his pain level was now even lower, at a level two, and he could no longer feel the metal in his neck. He even started poking around to find it, but he said he couldn't feel it. When he said that, I knew the angels had taken the metal out.

The meeting came to an end with both men promising to come back in the morning to report how they were doing. The next day the place was packed, as the whole facility had heard what happened. I brought both men up to testify again. By this time the first man had complete freedom of movement in his neck, with no pain at all. The second man was still pain-free, and even though he couldn't feel whether the metal in his neck and spine was gone, he knew he had experienced a miracle.

I mentioned that it would be cool if we could confirm the miracles with a metal detector. An officer who happened to be in the chapel that morning went and got one, and as he walked up on stage, he first tested it on his belt buckle to prove it worked. Then one by one he ran it over the two men. It didn't make a sound because there was now no metal in their bodies.

Some of the inmates still had trouble believing the miracle, so they followed both men into the chow hall because they knew they'd have to pass a metal detector before entering. Again, there was no sound. The metal was gone!

Seeing metal disappear from people's bodies has become a normal occurrence in my meetings. An inmate in a meeting had shrapnel stuck in his hand. As I prayed for the man's soul, the metal began to dissolve, and the bullet disappeared. This miracle was also verified by an officer who had a metal detector and was standing by. This is the magnitude of miracle you can expect to experience—and help bring about for others—when you are healed of the bents in your soul and no longer have anything in you that is in common with the enemy.

PRAYER ACTIVATION

Say the following prayers and decrees for healing and deliverance through the release of snow and hail. If you feel cold or get a vision or a dream that contains snow or hail, then know that you have been healed and delivered. If not, keep going. Declare your decrees, get into God's presence through worship, and then command the snow and hail to come again until you get your breakthrough.

Father, the Bible says that You have treasuries of snow and hail stored up for me to use in times of war and battle. Please open Your storehouse now! Go into the treasury and release those heavenly weapons against all my enemies.

I decree that huge hailstones and freezing snow are being dispatched to do battle for me against the evil spirits that are attached to my body, my soul, and every part of my life. Beat down Legion with this powerful heavenly weapon. Throw down huge rocks of ice on the heads of the giants, and kill more of them with the hail than with the sword!

I release the plague of hail against every spirit that is in my bloodline all the way back to Adam and forward to my descendants as well. I decree this plague will wipe out every demon god and goddess in my life, including the gods that are assaulting my family and me.

I decree Psalm 18 over myself. The Lord Almighty comes thundering from heaven to battle against my enemies, and when He speaks, hailstones and coals of fire scatter them and cause them to be totally vanquished!

I also loose Psalm 148 over every part of my life. When the Lord makes a decree that my enemies are to be destroyed, snow, hail, and all the heavens fulfill His word. In Jesus's name, amen.

CONCLUSION

I PRAY THAT YOU will use the revelation in this book to be set free from all soul wounds and receive and become all God has for you. Once you start experiencing soul healing through the power of Christ, your life will never be the same. You will walk in a new realm of supernatural power and provision.

In these pages I have given you principles for how to recognize soul wounds, identify the source of the wounds, and apply biblical and supernatural solutions that will bring healing and give new life. I believe that as you apply these principles, you will develop a more vibrant, effective prayer life; enjoy the abundant, prosperous life God longs to give you; and receive the blessings God is pouring out instead of continuing to suffer from the needless pain soul wounds are causing you.

You can walk in the fullness of the freedom Christ died to give us. He didn't sacrifice His life for you just so you could avoid hell and spend eternity with Him in heaven. He shed His blood and was resurrected from death so you could have new life in Him through His dunamis power. He wants you to be healed so you can live on this earth with true joy, peace, and happiness. I pray you will take the message of this book to heart. Let Him heal your soul so you can be set free!

NOTES

CHAPTER 1
WHY I COULDN'T CHANGE

1. *Tweeking* is the street term for using methamphetamines.

CHAPTER 2
THE WOUNDED SOUL

1. Thayer's Greek Lexicon, Electronic Database, Copyright © 2002, 2003, 2006, 2011 by Biblesoft, Inc., s.v. *"metamorphoó,"* accessed June 6, 2017, http://biblehub.com/greek/3339.htm.

2. Samuel Prideaux Treglles, *Gesenius's Hebrew-Chaldee Lexicon* (London: Samuel Bagster and Sons, Paternoster, Row, 1860).

3. Blue Letter Bible, s.v. *"syneidēsis,"* accessed June 5, 2017, https://www.blueletterbible.org/lang/lexicon/lexicon.cfm?Strongs=G4893&t=KJV.

4. Bible Hub, s.v. *"koilia,"* accessed June 5, 2017, http://biblehub.com/greek/2836.htm.

5. Blue Letter Bible, s.v. *"leb,"* accessed June 5, 2017, https://www.blueletterbible.org/lang/lexicon/lexicon.cfm?Strongs=H3820&t=KJV.

6. Blue Letter Bible, *"asthenēs,"* accessed June 8, 2017, https://www.blueletterbible.org/lang/Lexicon/Lexicon.cfm?strongs=G772&t=KJV.

7. Blue Letter Bible, s.v. *"sthenoō,"* https://www.blueletterbible.org/lang/Lexicon/lexicon.cfm?strongs=G4599&t=KJV.

CHAPTER 3
EFFECTS OF BEING WOUNDED

1. Blue Letter Bible, s.v. *"nephesh,"* accessed June 5, 2017, https://www.blueletterbible.org/lang/Lexicon/Lexicon.cfm?strongs=H5315&t=KJV.

2. Blue Letter Bible, s.v. *"kardia,"* accessed June 5, 2017, https://www.blueletterbible.org/lang/Lexicon/Lexicon.cfm?strongs=G2588&t=KJV.

3. Blue Letter Bible, s.v. "*euodoō*," accessed June 5, 2017, https://www.blueletterbible.org/lang/Lexicon/Lexicon.cfm?strongs=G2137&t=KJV.

4. Donna Jackson Nakazawa, "Childhood Trauma Leads to Life-long Chronic Illness—So Why Isn't the Medical Community Helping Patients?," Oath Inc., July 29, 2016, accessed June 20, 2017, http://www.huffingtonpost.com/donna-jackson-nakazawa/childhood-trauma-leads-to_b_11154082.html.

5. Blue Letter Bible, s.v. "*astheneia*," accessed June 5, 2017, https://www.blueletterbible.org/lang/Lexicon/Lexicon.cfm?strongs=G769&t=KJV.

6. Ibid.

7. Bible Hub, s.v. "*skotos*," accessed June 5, 2017, http://biblehub.com/thayers/4655.htm.

8. Bible Hub, s.v. "*ischyros*," accessed June 5, 2017, https://www.blueletterbible.org/lang/lexicon/lexicon.cfm?t=esv&strongs=g2478.

9. Bible Tools, s.v. "*ischuros*," Church of the Great God, accessed June 5, 2017, http://www.bibletools.org/index.cfm/fuseaction/Lexicon.show/ID/G2478/ischuros.htm.

Chapter 4
The Finished Work of Christ: The Cross

1. Blue Letter Bible, s.v. "*leb*."

2. Blue Letter Bible, s.v. "*dynatos*," accessed June 5, 2017, https://www.blueletterbible.org/lang/lexicon/lexicon.cfm?t=kjv&strongs=g1415.

3. "It is a law of nature that nothing can be in two places at the same time; and if sin was borne away by our Lord, it cannot rest upon us," from C. H. Spurgeon, *Spurgeon's Sermons on the Death and Resurrection of Jesus* (Peabody, MA: Hendrickson Publishers, 2005), 57.

4. Bible Hub, s.v. "*anapausis*," accessed June 6, 2017, http://biblehub.com/thayers/372.htm.

Chapter 5
The Finished Work of Christ: The Blood of Jesus

1. Blue Letter Bible, s.v. "*astheneia*."

2. Blue Letter Bible, s.v. "*syneidēsis*."

3. Blue Letter Bible, s.v. *"metanoeō,"* accessed June 6, 2017, http://www.blueletterbible.org/lang/Lexicon/Lexicon.cfm?strongs=G3340&t=KJV.

4. Blue Letter Bible, s.v. *"thanatos,"* accessed June 6, 2017, https://www.blueletterbible.org/lang/lexicon/lexicon.cfm?t=kjv&strongs=g2288.

Chapter 6
Dunamis Power

1. Blue Letter Bible, s.v. *"dynamis,"* accessed June 6, 2017, https://www.blueletterbible.org/lang/lexicon/lexicon.cfm?t=kjv&strongs=g1411.

2. Blue Letter Bible, s.v. *"astheneia."*

3. Bible Tools, s.v. *"ischuros."*

4. Blue Letter Bible, s.v. *"dynatos,"* accessed June 6, 2017, https://www.blueletterbible.org/lang/lexicon/lexicon.cfm?Strongs=G1415&t=KJV.

5. Blue Letter Bible, s.v. *"euodoō."*

Chapter 7
Premature Death and Bone Disease

1. "About Lyme Disease," LymeDisease.org, accessed June 6, 2017, https://www.lymedisease.org/lyme-basics/lyme-disease/about-lyme/.

2. Blue Letter Bible, s.v. *"astheneia."*

3. Ibid.

4. Blue Letter Bible, s.v. *"dynamis."*

5. Rose Eveleth, "There Are 37.2 Trillion Cells in Your Body," Smithsonian.com, October 24, 2013, accessed June 7, 2017, http://www.smithsonianmag.com/smart-news/there-are-372-trillion-cells-in-your-body-4941473/.

6. Blue Letter Bible, s.v. *"dynamis."*

Chapter 8
What Is Stopping the Flow?

1. Bible Study Tools, s.v. *"zao,"* http://www.biblestudytools.com/lexicons/greek/nas/zao.html.

2. Bible Hub, sv. *"shaar,"* accessed June 7, 2017, http://biblehub.com/hebrew/8179.htm; Bible Hub, s.v. *"pethach,"* accessed June 7, 2017, http://biblehub.com/hebrew/6607.htm.

3. Bible Study Tools, s.v. *"shaar,"* http://www.biblestudytools.com/lexicons/hebrew/kjv/shaar-2.html.

Chapter 9
Your Power Over Legion

1. Blue Letter Bible, s.v. *"sōphroneō,"* accessed June 7, 2017, https://www.blueletterbible.org/lang/lexicon/lexicon.cfm?t=esv&strongs=g4993.

2. *Sōphroneō* is from the root *sōphrōn*, which comes from the words *sōzō* (G4982) and *phrēn* (G5424), Blue Letter Bible, accessed June 7, 2017, https://www.blueletterbible.org/lang/Lexicon/lexicon.cfm?strongs=G4982&t=KJV, https://www.blueletterbible.org/lang/lexicon/lexicon.cfm?Strongs=G5424&t=KJV.

3. Bible Hub, s.v. *"mnēmeion,"* accessed June 7, 2017, http://biblehub.com/greek/3419.htm.

4. Bible Hub, s.v. *"katoikeō,"* accessed June 7, 2017, http://biblehub.com/greek/2730.htm.

5. Bible Hub, s.v. *"himation,"* accessed June 7, 2017, http://biblehub.com/greek/2440.htm.

Chapter 10
Soul Remedy for Eating Disorders

1. "The Health Effects of Overweight and Obesity," Centers for Disease Control, June 5, 2015, accessed June 20, 2017, https://www.cdc.gov/healthyweight/effects/index.html.

2. Bible Hub, s.v. *"nephesh,"* accessed June 7, 2017, http://biblehub.com/hebrew/5315.htm.

3. "What Causes an Eating Disorder?," The Center for Eating Disorders, accessed June 7, 2017, https://eatingdisorder.org/eating-disorder-information/underlying-causes/.

4. Blue Letter Bible, s.v. *"tsayid,"* accessed June 7, 2017, https://www.blueletterbible.org/lang/lexicon/lexicon.cfm?t=kjv&strongs=h6718.

5. Blue Letter Bible, s.v. *"'ayeph,"* accessed June 7, 2017, https://www.blueletterbible.org/lang/lexicon/lexicon.cfm?t=kjv&strongs=h5888.

6. Merriam-Webster Online, s.v. "languish," accessed June 7, 2017, https://www.merriam-webster.com/dictionary/languish.

Chapter 11
Character Bents

1. Blue Letter Bible, s.v. "*leb.*"

2. *The Book of Enoch* chapters 8 and 19, accessed June 7, 2017, http://wesley.nnu.edu/sermons-essays-books/noncanonical-literature /noncanonical-literature-ot-pseudepigrapha/book-of-enoch/; Flavius Josephus, *The Antiquities of the Jews* Book I chapter 3, accessed June 7, 2017, https://www.gutenberg.org/files/2848/2848-h/2848-h.htm#link 2HCH0003.

3. *The Book of Enoch* chapters 8 and 19; Flavius Josephus, *The Antiquities of the Jews* Book I chapter 3.

4. Blue Letter Bible, s.v. "*Qiysh,*" accessed June 7, 2017, https:// www.blueletterbible.org/lang/lexicon/lexicon.cfm?t=asv&strongs =h7027.

5. Blue Letter Bible, s.v. "'*el,*" accessed June 7, 2017, https://www .blueletterbible.org/lang/lexicon/lexicon.cfm?Strongs=H410.

6. *The American Heritage Dictionary,* s.v. "tea," accessed June 7, 2017, https://ahdictionary.com/word/search.html?q=teas.

7. Bible Hub, s.v. "*nephilim,*" accessed June 7, 2017, http://biblehub .com/hebrew/5303.htm.

8. Bible Hub, s.v. "*avah,*" accessed June 7, 2017, http://biblehub.com /hebrew/5753b.htm; Bible Study tools, s.v. "'*avah,*" accessed June 7, 2017, http://www.biblestudytools.com/lexicons/hebrew/nas/avah-3 .html.

9. Bible Hub, s.v. "*tapeinósis,*" accessed June 7, 2017, http:// biblehub.com/greek/5014.htm.

Chapter 12
Staying Free

1. Bible Hub, s.v. "*pale,*" accessed June 8, 2017, http://biblehub.com /greek/3823.htm.

2. Bethany Kochan, "Proper Percentage of Water in the Body," Leaf Group Ltd., updated May 11, 2015, accessed June 8, 2017, http:// www.livestrong.com/article/276984-proper-body-hydration -percentage/.

3. Flavius Josephus, *The Complete Works of Flavius Josephus* trans. William Whiston (London: T. Nelson and Sons, Paternoster Row, 1860), 136.

ABOUT THE AUTHOR

Katie Souza didn't always walk in the presence and power of God. In fact, for many years she lived a violent and drug-addicted life. Katie started experimenting with drugs as a teenager, and when her media career took off, her drug use escalated. She worked as a model and actress, but drugs caused her to lose job after job, so she turned further to crime to support herself.

Katie's life consisted of drugs, clandestine laboratories, stolen vehicles, high-speed chases, gun shoot-outs, and many arrests. When she was captured by federal marshals in February of 1999, she was at the end of her rope. Charged with manufacturing, conspiracy, and gun possession, Katie was sentenced to twelve and a half years in a federal prison.

The pressures of her circumstances finally drove her into the arms of God. As Katie began her long incarceration, the Holy Spirit gave her a hunger for the Word. Soon after, she started a Bible study within her cellblock. Then one night God told Katie she would have a new release date. Eighteen months later His word came to pass, and miraculously seven years were taken off of her sentence! (Her "out" date was the exact month and day God spoke to her. This is well-documented because she had announced the details to everyone she knew for months in advance!)

While still in prison Katie began writing her first book, *The Captivity Series: The Key to Your Expected End*, which is now in huge demand by inmates around the world. In late 2006 the Lord released a healing anointing upon Katie and her team. Since that time countless people have received miracles through her conferences and teaching resources. The Lord put a mandate on Katie to bring healing to His people through international media, and in 2013 Katie and her staff produced and debuted the video *Healing Your Soul: Real Keys to the Miraculous*, which can be seen around the globe on major networks and viewed on her website at www.katiesouza.com.

She and her husband, Robert, are now living out their *expected end* in Arizona.

CONNECT WITH US!

**CHARISMA
HOUSE**

(Spiritual Growth)

Facebook.com/CharismaHouse

@CharismaHouse

Instagram.com/CharismaHouse

SILOAM

(Health)

Pinterest.com/CharismaHouse

MODERN
ENGLISH
VERSION

(Bible)
www.mevbible.com